Make Your Own Cat Toys

Saving the Planet One Cat Toy at a Time

Text, design and illustrations © Holly Tse, 2008

ISBN-13: 978-1440462467
ISBN-10: 1440462461

FIRST EDITION

Book and cover design: Holly Tse
All photos by Holly Tse

Printed in the United States of America

Make Your Own Cat Toys
Saving the Planet One Cat Toy at a Time

Holly Tse

www.makeyourowncattoys.com

This book is dedicated to Mom

And in loving memory to Feely,
who taught our family to truly love cats

Contents

part one: getting started   1

In the Beginning   3
Safety First   8
Playing with Your Cat   15
Using this Book   19

part two: the cat toys   21

Toys Made from Packaging   23
Toys Made Out of Household Objects   53
Toys Made from Craft Materials   67
Toys Made Using Office and School Items   83
Toys Made from Old Clothing   93
How to Tie a Slip Knot   112

part three: a greener cat   115

Greener Toy Choices   116
Eco-friendly Cat Litter   117
Food for Thought   119
Other Products and Accessories   120

Index   123
About the Author   126

Part One:
Getting Started

In the Beginning

At the time, I didn't know that when I said, "Yes," to my boyfriend, how that one simple word would change my life forever.

I had been trying unsuccessfully for several months to become a "mom." However each time I visited the Humane Society, I left empty-handed.

The right kitten had yet to appear. In fact, adoptions were so brisk during the summer months that kittens were rarely available.

Thus, when my boyfriend called me to say he was at the Humane Society and they had kittens, I immediately answered, "Yes," when he asked if he should pick one out.

In my mind, I had always envisioned adopting a gentle grey tabby that would nestle in my arms and snooze peacefully under a sunbeam. What I didn't know was that my boyfriend had a completely different vision.

When I got home from work, instead of a soft, cuddly, fluffy grey ball of fur, I saw a wiry, dark creature who looked more like a bat than a cat with his sharp chin and pointed ears. His pupils were dilated like frying pans, but he was also purring like a banshee.

My boyfriend chose this kitten because, "All of the other kittens were sleeping in a corner, but this guy was really alert. He followed my every move with his eyes."

My boyfriend and I broke up about a month after the adoption, but Furball was a keeper.

Everyone who's ever had a kitten knows just how much energy they have. They race through rooms, pounce on unsuspecting feet, gnaw on things they shouldn't, and constantly demand your undivided attention.

Furball was all that and then some. He was 100% hyper-adrenaline 24/7. He lived and breathed to play every minute of the day. He would forsake food to play and he never slept when I was home, not even one wink during a 16 hour stretch. He played so hard that he would start panting, but then he would keep on going.

He was also very insistent on interactive play. It wasn't enough if I dangled a toy on a string in front of him. I had to make the toy behave like a mouse, hiding behind furniture, scurrying along the wall and slinking across the floor. If I didn't engage Furball, he would simply ignore the toy and latch his kitty claws and teeth into a much more interesting object, me.

Attempts at discipline were futile. He just had so much energy, he couldn't contain himself. Trying to tire him out was like attempting to put out the sun with a bucket of water. I tried introducing "calm time" by sitting very still and eliminating all distractions. As I

100% hyper-adrenaline 24/7

sat statue-like on the floor, all was serene for about five seconds, until I blinked. The next thing I knew, a ball of black fur was hurtling towards my eyelid with outstretched claws.

Well-meaning friends with cats told me that Furball would calm down after about six months. He didn't. They said I would notice a difference when he was a year old. A year passed and he was still hyperactive.

After two years however, I finally did notice a change in Furball. That was when he began to act like a normal three month old kitten.

During his formative years, I found myself visiting pet stores with alarming frequency as I desperately scoured the shelves for new toys that would hold his interest.

A rare moment of calm

In fact, during Furball's first month at home, I easily cleared out the local chain store. I even got suckered into buying the pom-pom on a spring nailed to a board, which looked fun to a human, but was deadly dull to a high energy kitten.

As I cast my net further to include specialty pet boutiques, Furball became one spoiled little cat. He had his own toy box for the assortment of balls, springs, feathers, bells, rattling mice, woolly shapes, catnip pouches, fur-covered fake rodents, and numerous other toys. In the back of my mind, I was somewhat disturbed at this amassment of toys. I also couldn't help but notice the ubiquitous "Made in (insert faraway country name here)" sticker on most of the toys.

I wish I could say that I had an overnight green epiphany where I renounced toy buying, but Furball's insistence on playing 24/7 drove me to desperate measures. No new toys meant claws and teeth relentlessly attaching themselves to my pant leg day and night. However, the plethora of cat toys was at odds with my lifelong environmentalism and especially incongruent with my job at World Wildlife Fund where I was working to save the environment. I knew I had to find new ways to entertain him.

I began closely examining toys from a cat perspective. What would interest a cat? A crunchy rustle, a paw-sized delight, the right amount of stuffing for sinking in claws and teeth. What would induce indifference?

Primary colors, surfaces that were uncomfortable for delicate paws to touch, large objects that were too big for a cat.

I also noticed that there seemed to be an inverse relationship between the cost of a toy and the cat's interest in said toy. The more expensive and complicated an item was, the less likely the cat would want to play with it. In fact, it seemed like the high-priced toys were designed to appeal to the humans buying them rather than to the cat.

Cats weren't interested in these costly complicated items. They were much more intrigued by the crunchy bag they came in.

As I honed my cat perspective, I could accurately predict which toys would be a hit and which ones would be a flop. I also developed a knack for choosing toys for other people's cats and dogs. Friends and family would tell me that the gifts I had given their pets had become their furry friend's favorite toy.

Furball was always up to something, in this case, the top of the bathroom door.

As I figured out what cats would like, I realized that many of the toys could be recreated at home from cast-off items. Soon, it became a natural extension for me to deconstruct toys and experiment with everyday things around the house to make my own cat toys. Besides saving a lot of money and minimizing Furball's carbon paw print, I could create something in a matter of minutes for those times when Furball demanded something new and exciting.

The first toy I invented for Furball was the Flippity Flappity Flag. It was a runaway success. He loved it so much that he would chase it in circles until he fell over from dizziness and then he would immediately get up to chase it some more. After that first toy, dozens more followed over the years until I had quite the compendium of toys. I'm also very grateful to friends who shared their toy ideas with me.

Furball didn't begin to slow down until he was three years old. Now, at a healthy seven years of age, he still loves to play. He will always be my eternal kitten.

It is my sincere wish to share with you the joy of making your own cat toys and saving the planet one cat toy at a time. Obviously, the claim about saving the planet is a bit facetious, but if you consider that there are over 60 million cats in American households, reducing the resources and waste of even a single toy per cat could make a huge difference.

I also hope that you and your beloved cat (or cats) will enjoy many hilarious and fun moments with your new toys made from old stuff.

A special message from Furball

Mommy thought I would be the best spokesperson (or spokescat) to talk to you about the importance of safety. You probably want to start making toys right now and might skip reading the chapter about safety. I'm here to say, "DON'T SKIP IT!"

Safety First

By the power vested in all cats to rule their owners, I command you to read this safety chapter before making any toys. Also, fetch me some tasty fish snacks and give me a belly rub while you're at it.

If you love your Kitty as much as Mommy loves me, please follow the Make Your Own Cat Toys Safety Commandments.

The Safety Commandments:

1. If kids are small, then not at all.
2. If in doubt, leave it out.
3. To set the right tone, don't let Kitty play alone.
4. If Kitty tries to eat it, the toy has got to beat it.
5. If it falls apart, toss and restart.

I will now explain the Safety Commandments. In my cat greatness, I command you to read them all.

Commandment #1
If kids are small, then not at all.

If you have young children in your home, put this book away until your kids are old enough to know not to eat things off the ground or put things in their mouths. Come to think of it, dogs do this too. Therefore, you should NEVER have cat toys lying around where young children (or not too bright dogs) can access them.

Cat Toys + Young Kids = Bad Combination

Mommy saw on TV that a general rule of thumb is that anything that can fit through a toilet paper roll is a choking hazard. That covers many of the toys in this book, and for that matter, most cat toys too. Thus, this book is not suitable for homes with young children.

As well, when older children are making toys from this book, they should always be supervised by a parent or guardian. Some of the toys require sharp objects such as scissors, pinking shears, knitting and sewing needles or a sewing machine. The adult who knows the child best should decide whether these activities are appropriate.

Commandment #2
If in doubt, leave it out.

Mommy invented these toys for me. She knows how I play and what I can't resist chewing on. Therefore, while all of these toys are safe for me, they might not be appropriate for your Kitty.

There are over 60 million cats in homes across the United States. As much as I love Mommy and think she's brilliant for bringing me breakfast and dinner, she simply can't predict how every cat in the world will react to each and every toy. Cats are unique individuals in terms of food, be-havior and personality. Toys are no exception.

Some cats are short a few crayons in their crayon box and will eat things that are not good for them. Others, are simply too curious or too young to know any better. That's why your Kitties are depending on YOU to know better. Only you know your cat's personality and quirks and whether a toy is appropriate. Your Kitty needs you to use your best judgment.

If you think a toy might be a risk, don't make it. There are over 50 toys in this book, so you have plenty of others to choose from.

Commandment #3
Set the right tone, don't let Kitty play alone.

I will let you in on a little feline secret. As independent as we mighty cats are, we need the humans in our lives. The toys in this book are designed for you to play with us.

So, when you're giving Kitty any of these toys, make sure she's supervised by a responsible adult. If that happens to be you, always watch your cat closely when playing with all cat toys, not just the ones in this book.

Commandment #4
If Kitty tries to eat it, the toy has got to beat it.

Because you are closely supervising your cat, you will notice if he or she tries to eat a toy. If this is the case, you should immediately remove the toy and dispose of it. Since most of the toys in this book take only minutes to make and are constructed from things that were going to be recycled or thrown out, it's not a big deal to get rid of a toy. It's always better to be safe.

When we cats eat something yucky, we can't spit it out because our tongues have little barbs on them. So, we keep on eating. That's how seemingly harmless objects can become harmful. If we ingest them, they may tangle in our intestines and that would be very very bad.

Besides, we would much rather eat a tasty treat than a toy.

Commandment #5
If it falls apart, toss and restart.

Toys that become soiled and worn could be potentially unsafe and therefore, should be thrown out. Besides, how can you expect royalty to play with dirty broken toys? Your Kitty deserves better. The unwritten commandment is that you must then make us a replacement toy.

Special Commandment
Avoid the hurt by playing alert.

This special commandment is for your safety.

I hate to admit that I have accidentally scratched and bitten Mommy while playing. She's not very happy about it, but this usually happens when she's not paying close attention.

I can't help myself when I get so excited. Sometimes I misjudge just how far away she is and grab her instead of the toy. Mommy can usually see by my dilated pupils that I am in "crazy mode" and that's when she knows to either stop playing or to redirect my attention by throwing a toy far away for me to chase.

You can make yourself and your Kitty feel better by playing alertly to avoid unfortunate accidents.

That's it for now!

Thanks for listening to me, but since I'm a cat, you really had no choice but to listen. Use your common sense and play safe, play smart, and play fun. OK, on to the toys!

Your pal,
Furball

Fortune 8 Cat
Keep an eye out for me throughout this book. I'll let you know of any special safety concerns for a toy.

Playing With Your Cat

Cats are curious creatures and contrary to common misconceptions by non-cat people, they are also very social animals. Kitty appreciates and delights in your company, especially when it's playtime.

Some cats, especially kittens, love to play all day, while others will rouse from their 18 hour naps for only a few minutes of lazy swatting. Despite this wide variation, there is one common denominator at the very heart of why cats play and that's instinct.

So, all you need to do is think like a cat hunting for its prey and you'll be the ultimate playtime companion for your Kitty. It's as simple as repeating this mantra:

Think like a cat. See like a cat. Hear like a cat. Play like a cat.

Imagine you're about a foot tall, meandering lazily through a grassy field. What does the grass feel like between your toes? It's soft and has a satisfying give under your paws.

You freeze. What caught your attention? Was it the tiny rustle of a mouse (mmm yummy) or the sudden movement of a bird's wing zinging past your peripheral vision? You pause.

You hear the rustling again, so you wait and listen intently. All of your attention is focused on this one tiny sound.

You are rewarded when your eyes spot the slightest movement of a single blade of grass only a few feet ahead of you. You wait. Slowly, ever so slowly, the rustling sound gets closer and closer to you.

Your body tenses up and your muscles coil like a tightly wound spring. Suddenly, you release all of that stored energy as you explosively pounce onto a poor unfortunate mouse. What happens next is up to your imagination and personal belief systems. No creatures were harmed in the writing of this paragraph, but you do get the point, right?

Kitty is attracted to rustling, scratching noises as they resemble little creatures visiting for dinner. Movement and motion catches Kitty's eyes because for some unknown reason, the dinner guests always seem to be in a hurry when passing by her.

The more a toy sounds, appears and behaves like dinner, the more your Kitty will enjoy it. Since toys are generally inanimate objects, it's up to you to animate them. To help you make playtime even more fun, Furball gives tips and suggestions throughout this book.

As well, the toys have been grouped into one or more different play categories. Perhaps your Kitty likes to jump as high as she can, maybe she's a sprinter, or she just might prefer to patiently stalk her toys. Whatever her fancy happens to be, you'll be able to select a toy from a play category that suits her mood in the moment.

The Play Categories

1. Catch

These toys encourage Kitty to leap straight up into the air and pretend that she's snaring a bird, bug or butterfly between her paws. If your Kitty is a natural jumper and can snatch toys out of the air like a World Cup soccer goalie, then this play category is perfect for her.

It's also especially ideal for kittens and high energy cats as the vertical leaping helps to burn off excess energy. Simply toss the toy above Kitty's head and watch how high she leaps.

2. Chase

What playful Kitty can resist tearing across a room at full speed in pursuit of her prey? For agile cats who like to run, these toys have enough weight to gather speed when thrown, but they're still small and nimble enough to present a fun challenge for your cat.

All you need to do is slide one of these toys across the floor, and Kitty will imagine it's a small mouse scurrying away. How can she resist?

3. Stalk

Cats are natural hunters and these toys give Kitty a chance to practice her hunting skills. She can also hone her concealment skills as she creeps up on her prey.

While you may be able to clearly see her butt sticking out of the box she's hiding in, humor her and pretend that she is invisible. You'll also have to pretend that you don't notice her tail swishing back and forth.

Toys in this play category are designed to be hidden and to appear and disappear. Kitty will wait patiently for the "hidden" toy to make its presence known. She's humoring you too as she knows that the toy is right behind the couch. It won't be too long before she springs into action and pounces for the kill.

The key to "stalk" toys is your participation in making the "prey" come alive. Hide the toy, rustle it, move it out of Kitty's sight. Wait as patiently as she does. For Kitty, the fun is in the waiting.

4. Wrestle

These toys allow Kitty to test her strength, much like she did when she was a small kitten wrestling with her siblings to elbow them out at meal-time. Wrestling also provided practice at taking down her prey and delivering the final blow.

Kitty will grasp the toy tightly in her paws and jaws and dig furiously with her hind legs. Or, she might hang on and play a game of tug-of-war with you. Tickle her tummy with the toy and watch how quickly she grabs on and refuses to let go.

5. Lazy Cat

Finally, there are toys for the cat who is winding down his or her play level. After a good run, Kitty might still want to play, but is feeling lazy.

With these toys, she can lie on her back and swat half-heartedly in the air. Even Furball has Lazy Cat moments.

Using this Book

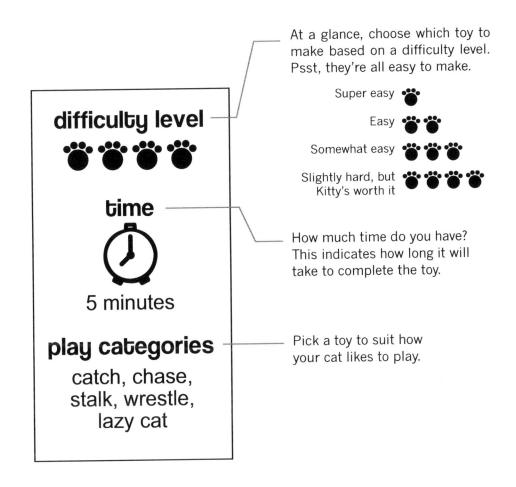

At a glance, choose which toy to make based on a difficulty level. Psst, they're all easy to make.

Super easy

Easy

Somewhat easy

Slightly hard, but Kitty's worth it

How much time do you have? This indicates how long it will take to complete the toy.

Pick a toy to suit how your cat likes to play.

difficulty level

time

5 minutes

play categories

catch, chase, stalk, wrestle, lazy cat

Part Two:
The Cat Toys

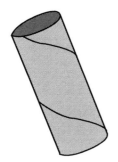

Candy Rocket

Schrodinger's Box

Peek-a-boo House

Ring Toss

Sweep Around

Classic Shopping Bag

The Pretzel

Braided Rope Snake

Floppy Jacks

Flying Horseshoes

Tape Ball

Hide 'n Peek Bag

Flippity Flappity Flag

Juice Pull

Juicy Hoop

Madcap

Water Bottle Dodgeball

Crunch and Bunch

Tubular Tubes

Tissue Kebab

Unwrap This!

Cat Toys Made from Packaging

Candy Rocket

The Candy Rocket will send Kitty flying to the moon. It's a sweet treat that she'll enjoy to her heart's content – the perfect guilt-free indulgence for you and Kitty.

Simply launch the Candy Rocket into the air and watch Kitty take off after it.

What you'll need:

Corrugated cardboard

1 shoelace

Scissors

Oh dahling, you shouldn't have!

1. Cut a 10" x 1" strip out of the cardboard.

2. Cut the strip into ten 1" squares. They do not have to be perfect in size or shape.

3. Fold one of the squares in half and make two small cuts in the center to create a small hole. See Figure 1. Tip: It's easier to fold the cardboard parallel to the grooves rather than against them.

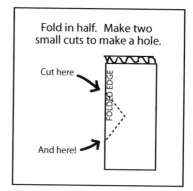

Fold in half. Make two small cuts to make a hole.

Cut here

FOLDED EDGE

And here!

Figure 1

Furball's Meow

Run your thumbnail along the edges of the Candy Rocket and I'll hear that you're ready to play.

4. Unfold the square and trim it into a circle with the scissors. The cardboard shape doesn't need to be a perfect circle. The goal is to soften the hard edges and corners.

5. Repeat for the other circles.

6. Tie a double knot at one end of the shoelace.

7. Thread the circles onto the shoelace to form a stack. When the stack is about 1" high, tie a knot at the other end of the shoelace to hold the pieces together. See Figure 2.

8. Cut off the extra shoelace and the Candy rocket is now fired up and ready for Kitty to eat it up. That's figuratively speaking, not literal!!!

Thread cardboard onto the shoelace.

Figure 2

"I love cats because I love my home, and after a while they become its visible soul."

- Jean Cocteau

Schrodinger's Box

Schrodinger's Cat is a quantum physics theory that has something to do with a cat in a box and the act of observation affecting what state the cat is in.

Of course, this is a simplification of his theory, but if you have a cat and you have a box, you don't need to look inside to know that your cat is having a merry time inside the box.

While cats aren't too particular when it comes to boxes, some boxes are definitely more fun than others. Kitty will love a box that is slightly taller than her. If it's just a little too tall to peek inside, she won't be able to resist!

The perfect box lets Kitty stand inside easily and turn around. Kitty wants to feel like she has found a secret hiding place that's cozy, but not cramped. A moving box is just the right size. Plus, it's durable and you can recycle it after Kitty has worn it out. If the box still has flaps, it's even more intriguing.

Moving boxes can also be flattened and discreetly hidden when uppity guests stop by, but of course, this wouldn't apply to you because all of your friends love cats.

What you'll need:

1 corrugated cardboard box (as close to "perfect" as possible)

1. Place the box on the floor with the opening facing to the side. You can also push the box flaps into the box, but leave enough space for your cat to walk in.

2. To mix it up, place the box right side up with the opening at the top. Kitty will want to see what's inside and might just hop in!

Furball's Meow

Throw a small toy into the box and watch me chase after it. Hide a dangling toy behind the box and my natural stalking instincts will kick in.

"Cats are intended to teach us that not everything in nature has a purpose."

- Garrison Keillor

Peek-a-boo House

To Kitty, the Peek-a-boo House is as grand as any palatial mansion in Beverly Hills, maybe even grander. Unlike the typical Hollywood extravagance, in this case, less is more. Less box is more fun. Cut out pieces of the box to create custom architectural elements that will make Kitty feel like a pampered movie star. Kitty's new eco-friendly home will make even Ed Begley, Jr. green with envy.

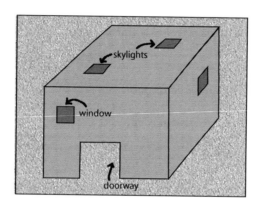

What you'll need:

1 corrugated cardboard box, about the size of a typical moving box (18" x 14" x 12") or a copy paper box

Box cutter or a strong pair of scissors

Furball's Meow

Take one of my wand toys and insert it through a window or paw slit. Give the toy a wiggle and see if you can pull it away faster than I can swat it.

This is way better than a $10 million home. If only I had a private chef.

1. If the box has flaps, cut them off. Flip the box upside down. Now, your Peek-a-boo House has a roof, but it needs a door.

2. Cut a doorway. Kitty will prefer a modest entrance, just big enough for her to easily sneak in, but not too snug as she wouldn't want to ruffle her fur.

3. Following the tradition of Boo-haus style architecture, Kitty's home should also have peek-a-boo style windows. Cut two to four windows on the sides of the box at different levels. Each window should be slightly bigger than the size of your cat's paws, but not so big that he or she can see easily out of the window.

4. Add one or two skylights by cutting holes in the "roof" of the box. Follow the size guidelines for windows.

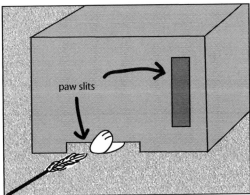

Human Suggests

If Kitty insists on having a "McMansion," simply add more boxes with their doorways facing each other. Since you're using old boxes, this is one McMansion expansion that you can feel good about.

5. Now for the ultimate cat home feature that has no human equivalent: the paw slit. On one wall, cut a 3" x 1" rectangle at the base of the box. You can also cut a 6" x 2" vertical rectangle to increase the curb (and play) appeal of Kitty's home.

6. Take a small piece of scrap cardboard and run its edge along the sides of the doorway, windows, skylights and paw slits to smooth out any rough spots. The Peek-a-boo House is now ready for Kitty to move in.

Ring Toss

Ring Toss isn't just for county fairs and backyard BBQs. Now, Kitty can join the circle of fun when you bring the carnival indoors.

This toy is ideal when Kitty has an endless supply of energy because you can easily make an endless supply of rings in seconds.

You'll be the one to toss the rings, but Kitty will be taking home the top prize as she flaunts her agility and lightning reflexes.

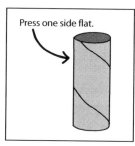

Press one side flat.

Figure 1

What you'll need:

1 toilet paper or paper towel roll

Scissors

1. Lightly press the toilet paper roll flat so that you can cut it easily with scissors. See Figure 1.

2. Cut a ring approximately 1/4" thick. See Figure 2.

3. Continue cutting as many rings as you or Kitty desires. It's now time to play Ring Toss and the more rings you make, the merrier the fun.

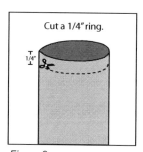

Cut a 1/4" ring.

1/4"

Figure 2

Furball's Meow

Mommy gets in close to toss a ring over my head and I leap up to catch it between my paws. As soon as my feet touch the ground, I'm ready for the next Ring Toss.

Sweep Around

If your Kitty is like Furball and attacks the broom while you're sweeping, it's time to make her a Kitty-sized broom to call her own. Sweep Around will make your spring cleaning a little easier as Kitty frolics out of your way. Please note that Sweep Around does not do windows or toilets.

What you'll need:

1 toilet paper roll

Scissors

1. Cut one end of the toilet paper roll to make parallel lengthwise strips. See Figure 1. The strips should be about 2.5" long (just past the half-way mark) and 0.3" wide. Cut all the way around the roll. This will form the bristle end of the broom.

2. Press the toilet paper roll flat. Then, fold it in half lengthwise. Fold it in half lengthwise one more time.

3. Fluff up the sweeper bristles so that it fans out like a broom. Sweep Around is now ready to sweep Kitty off her feet.

Cut strips all the way around.

Figure 1

Furball's Meow

Mommy dusts the carpet with the Sweep Around and the rustling sound it makes is just like a little mouse.

It doesn't clean the carpet very well though. Sometimes humans are weird.

Classic Shopping Bag

The mysterious allure of a shopping bag beckons Kitty with a magnetism much greater than anything that could possibly be inside.

While she may turn her nose up at the bag's contents, she'll light up like a girl opening a Tiffany's box when you set the bag down on the floor. Be sure to select a "classic" bag that is worthy of Kitty's exquisite taste.

What you'll need:

1 large paper shopping bag – You've probably already switched to a reusable tote, but now you finally have a use for all of those shopping bags that you've been saving for years.

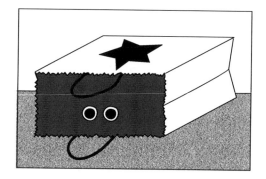

1. Open the shopping bag with a flourish so that Kitty knows this bag is for her.

2. Place the bag on the floor with the opening facing to the side. That's it!

Furball's Meow

When I'm inside the Classic Shopping Bag, take a pen (with the cap on) and tap the bag on all sides. The loud popping crunch created by my paws swatting the bag is a symphony to my ears.

The Pretzel

This sure beats a ballgame!

The Pretzel is creative recycling at its best. You can feel good about getting even more play mileage from a shopping bag by reincarnating the bag's handles as another cat toy.

If you don't have any bags, ask a girlfriend. She's sure to have one and will be glad to reduce some clutter from her home. This might also be a good time to show her how amazing your trendy reusable tote is.

After removing the bag handles, you can use the paper bag as a cat toy or as a creative way to wrap gifts for your friends.

What you'll need:

2 handles from a paper shopping bag – The handles should be the stiff twine-like ones, commonly used in many retail store bags.

1. Remove the handles from the bag. Cut off the ends above the adhesive glue. Dispose of the adhesive ends.

2. Tie one handle into a knot. Tie it again to secure the knot.

3. Take the second handle and tie it to the first handle. Randomly weave the ends through the loops made by the first handle.

4. Weave or tie any ends sticking out so that the two handles are joined together. There's no need to be precise as Kitty will appreciate your efforts regardless of what the final product looks like. You're done. It's time to start the food fight with the Pretzel.

Furball's Meow

Meow! For a fun time, hold one end of the Pretzel and shake it to get my attention. Throw it high and I'll catch it. Throw it far and I'll give chase.

Braided Rope Snake

Don't be alarmed if a Braided Rope Snake slithers into Kitty's playground. Kitty's not scared. She'll pounce on it like a mongoose.

This crafty snake takes only minutes to make, and it takes even less time to endear itself in Kitty's heart.

What you'll need:

2 pieces of rope approximately 1/8" to 1/4" thick and 60" long – A great source of repurposed rope is the drawstring from a sack-style shopping bag.

1. Tie the first rope directly around the middle of the second rope to form an "X" that is uniform on all sides. See Figure 1.

2. Take the ends of the second rope and reinforce the "X" by knotting them around the middle as well.

3. Grab one end of the rope (it doesn't matter which one) and hold it up in the air so that the other three ends hang downwards. See Figure 2.

4. Braid the three hanging ends until there are only 3" to 4" of unbraided rope remaining.

Furball's Meow

I love it when Mommy makes the Braided Rope Snake act like a real snake. She slithers it on the ground and whips it up like it's about to strike. That's when I leap high and wrestle it down.

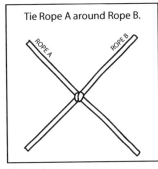

Tie Rope A around Rope B.

ROPE A

ROPE B

Figure 1

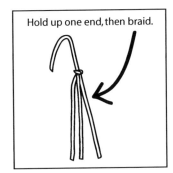

Hold up one end, then braid.

Figure 2

5. To finish off the braid, tie two of the unbraided rope ends together. Then knot the third end to one of the other two ends.

6. Continue tying the ends to each other two to three times until it feels like the snake will not come undone. Symmetry and perfection are not important. In fact, the more asymmetrical the end is, the more appealing it will be to Kitty. The Rope Snake is now finished.

"Some people say that cats are sneaky, evil, and cruel. True, and they have many other fine qualities as well."

- Missy Dizick

Floppy Jacks

Floppy Jacks are great for cats who love to leap and catch things mid-air. The Floppy Jacks' knotted center gives it some heft for acceleration and its floppy appendages are irresistible eye candy for Kitty.

What you'll need:

2 handles from a shopping bag – The handles should be the rope-style handles used in fancy retail bags, both plastic and paper.

1. Remove the rope handles from the bag. Usually rope handles are knotted to keep them from pulling through the bag and you should be able to easily untie them. However, if the ropes have been sealed with glue to prevent fraying, simply cut the rope above the adhesive and dispose of the adhesive ends.

2. Cut the rope so that you have four pieces that are each approximately 4" long.

3. Take one piece of rope and tie it around the middle of a second piece of rope. This will form an "X" that is fairly uniform on all sides.

4. Then, take the second piece of rope and reinforce the "X" by knotting it around the middle of the first piece of rope.

5. Repeat steps 3 and 4 with the other two pieces of rope. You now have a pair of Floppy Jacks.

Furball's Meow

I love Floppy Jacks. They're like a bird flapping its wings, only floppier and made of rope, and without the feathers, chirping and pecking.

Flying Horseshoes

A game of horseshoes harkens back to simpler times with laid back companionship, grassroots skill and a little bit of lady luck.

Well, it's time for you and your Kitty partner to fire up some down home fun with Flying Horseshoes. They're a quick and dirty use of shopping bag handles. Kitty will go from a lazy cantor to a full gallop before you can say, "Giddy-up!"

What you'll need:

Stiff rope handles from paper shopping bag – These should be the twine-like handles.

Scissors

1. Cut the handles from the paper shopping bag. Be sure to cut off and dispose of the adhesive part that attaches to the bag. You'll now have two horseshoes ready to toss. Hold both loosely in one hand at the bottom of the U-shape, then give a shake and toss.

"Never underestimate the power of a purr."
- Anonymous

Furball's Meow

I reckon if you throw both at the same time, I'll have more fun than a fat-bellied coyote in a henhouse.

Tape Ball

Turn a potentially sticky situation into a ball of fun. Tape Ball brings back the nostalgia of schoolyard days when you would collect elastic bands until you had enough to make a big rubber ball.

It's time to start collecting again, only this time, you'll be collecting adhesive tape.

Packing tape and masking tape work best to create the cat equivalent of a volleyball.

What you'll need:

Used packing or masking tape, collected from packages and gifts.
It will take a long time to collect enough tape, so start now :).

1. Carefully peel the tape from the paper.

2. Roll it onto itself to form a ball shape.

3. Repeat as you come across used tape until you form a ball that is about 3/4" in diameter. Once it reaches this size, Tape Ball is ready to be served to Kitty.

Furball's Meow

Mommy sometimes pretends that the Tape Ball is a soccer ball and I'm the goalie. She never gets the ball past me. I'm too fast.

Fortune 8 Cat
Make sure the sticky side of the tape is not facing outwards on the Tape Ball. If your cat is a weirdo and likes to lick adhesives, take Tape Ball away from him or her.

Hide 'n Peek Bag

Cats love flowers as much as we do. This is evidenced by the constant Kitty chatter when a bouquet arrives. She'll follow you around like her one true love in the hopes of nibbling on a delicate petal.

Help keep your flowers safely away from Kitty by distracting her with the Hide 'n Peek Bag. It's a source of amusement that you can create in 60 seconds or less.

What you'll need:

Plastic bag from a bouquet of flowers – This is the triangular bag with a hole at the bottom for the stems and an opening at the top for the flowers.

3 to 4 of your cat's favorite toys

1. Unbelievably easy. Open the flower bag. If it's closed on one or both ends, cut the ends off so that a tube is formed.

2. Place your cat's toys inside the bag. That's it!

Human Suggests

If you don't have a flower bag, drop hints to that special someone that you'd like some flowers. "It's for the cat, really." Or, why not buy some for yourself? You deserve a treat.

Furball's Meow

Can I eat your flowers? No? Ok, how about taking a wand toy and sliding it into one end of the flower bag to poke my toys around? What a fun game that will be!

Flippity Flappity Flag

Kitty may not have expressed any prior interest in patriotism. However, the Flippity Flappity Flag, with its crisp snapping sounds and wildly erratic movements will have her standing at attention in no time.

Selecting the right plastic bag is key to creating this toy. The bag should be made from a crisp and heavy plastic.

To test the bag for effectiveness, do the "symphony test." Place an object in the bag, go to the symphony and then take the object out of the bag. If everyone around you gives you nasty looks, then this is ideal Flippity Flappity Flag material.

After you've reused your bags multiple times and they're too dodgy for groceries and full of too many holes to be used for garbage (especially cat litter), you can use them for cat toys. In an ideal world, everyone would carry reusable totes and I would have to invent new toys because plastic bags would no longer exist. I'm looking forward to Make Your Own Cat Toys Part II.

What you'll need:

Plastic bag

Heavy shoelace

Scissors

1. Cut a 5" x 1.5" rectangle from the plastic bag.

2. Tie a slip knot at the end of the shoelace. See page 112 for instructions on how to tie a slip knot.

3. Slip about 1" of the plastic bag through the loop in the shoelace. Pull tightly to secure the shoelace around the plastic bag. Flippity Flappity Flag is now ready to be waved.

"I have noticed that what cats most appreciate in a human being is not the ability to produce food which they take for granted – but his or her entertainment value."

- Geoffrey Household

Furball's Meow

Hold on to the end of the shoelace and wave your arms in big circles over your head. I can't resist the frantic waving of the Flippity Flappity Flag with its sweet melodic snapping sound.

Plus, when you flap your arms, you look really silly, but you'll be having way too much fun to care.

play categories

catch,
lazy cat

Juice Pull

Juice Pull is by far, the "make your own" toy known and loved by Kitty parents everywhere. It's the quintessential example of garbage being universally fascinating to our furry feline friends.

The curly plastic pull tab from a juice carton is so appealing because it's paw-sized and wiggly-jiggly. (There's a reason why you don't need a Ph.D. to invent cat toys.)

So, next time you're opening up a carton of OJ, see the world with creative cat eyes and save that plastic tab for some refreshing fun.

What you'll need:

Plastic pull tab from a carton of juice

1 shoelace

1. Open the juice container and remove the plastic tab that seals in the freshness. Be sure to wash the plastic tab.

2. Tie the shoelace securely to the tab and you're good to go.

Furball's Meow

So simple. Just dangle it in front of me. Drink the juice to get your vitamin C, which must stand for "cat" since it's good for you.

Juicy Hoop

The inspiration for Juicy Hoop was a pricey cat toy. Finicky Furball didn't care much for the toy dangling on the string. However, he was extremely fascinated by the plastic ring on the other end.

Juicy Hoop is unique in this book because you don't set out to make this toy. Rather, you go about your day-to-day activities and chance upon the perfect plastic ring. So, keep your eyes and your mind open to possibilities. The next time you have a bottle of juice or some other beverage, take a closer look at the container and see if it contains the ultimate Juicy Hoop waiting to be released.

What you'll need:

1 plastic ring, commonly found on plastic juice or beverage bottles, and also on plastic jugs

1 shoelace

1. Wash the plastic ring to remove any traces of the beverage.

2. To play catch with Kitty, wave the ring to get her attention and then toss it in the air.

3. To play chase or "stalking," tie the shoelace to the plastic ring. Make a double knot to reinforce it. Juicy Hoop is now ready to entertain Kitty.

Furball's Meow

To pique my interest and stimulate my stalking instincts, drag Juicy Hoop behind objects so that it's hidden from my view. Watch me crouch low and flick my tail as I prepare to POUNCE!

Madcap

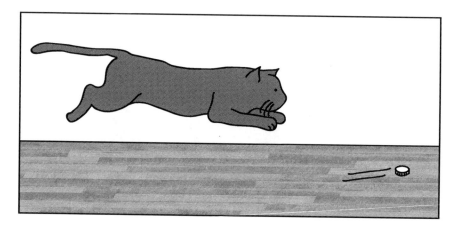

Don't be fooled by Madcap's simplicity. This plastic bottle cap may seem ho-hum to us humans, but Kitty will go mad for it. She'll be a spitfire demon running around the room like a mad hatter. It's mad-cap, crazy chasin' fun for everyone.

What you'll need:

1 plastic bottle cap, approximately 1" in diameter

1. Recycle the bottle, but keep the cap. Wash and rinse well.

2. Place the top of the cap on a hard surface such as kitchen tiles, hardwood or linoleum. Slide the cap on the floor like an air hockey paddle to attract Kitty's attention.

3. When her interest is piqued, send the Madcap sliding quickly across the room.

Furball's Meow

Sometimes Mommy's lazy when it's time to play. She thinks I don't notice that she keeps a stash of Madcaps handy so that she can re-main seated while I run around the room.

Water Bottle Dodgeball

Admittedly, Water Bottle Dodgeball is much more entertaining for the humans than it is for Kitty.

Nevertheless, the water bottle's wobbly movements will pique Kitty's curiosity. Just remember to roll the bottle gently and slowly. When Kitty's tired of this game, she'll let you know. Afterwards, be sure to reward her with a treat for being such a good sport. If your Kitty is the nervous type, it's better to skip this game.

Of all the indignities...

What you'll need:

1 16.9 fl. oz. (500mL) water bottle with a regular cap, not the sport cap

1 cup of water

1. Fill the water bottle halfway with water.

2. Screw the cap on TIGHTLY.

3. Place the bottle on the ground and GENTLY roll it towards Kitty. She'll trot out of the way to avoid it. Repeat until Kitty is tired of the game—she'll let you know. If in doubt, stop playing.

Furball's Meow

I don't really understand what's going on, but Mommy seems to really enjoy this game. So, I'll humor her for a few rolls of the bottle, but she's smart enough to know to quit while she's ahead.

time

1 minute

play categories
catch, chase

Crunch and Bunch

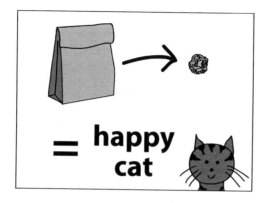

= **happy cat**

After lunch

Crunch and bunch

To make the Crunch and Bunch

No, that's not a weird haiku, but it does show you how simple it is to make this toy out of a used lunch bag. Although you're probably already packing your lunch in reusable totes to cut down on waste, sometimes you'll still receive the occasional paper bag. Fortunately, they make such a fantastic cat toy that Kitty will be begging you to brown bag it more often.

What you'll need:

Brown paper lunch bag, or any other bag made from thin paper

1. Cut a 6" x 8" rectangle out of the paper bag.

2. Crumple the paper into a tight ball. Voila! You've just created a Crunch and Bunch.

Furball's Meow

Try different sizes of paper. I like the bigger balls for catching and the smaller ones for swatting around the room.

Tubular Tubes

Like, ohmigod, it doesn't get any easier than this. Tubular Tubes is soooo awesome because it's like, soooo easy to make. For sure, Kitty will love it. You, like, take something that's so totally boring and like, cut it up, and ohmigod, you have so many Tubular Tubes.

What you'll need:

1 thick drinking straw, 1/4" to 1/2" in diameter – Bubble tea (aka Boba or pearl tea) straws are ideal.

1. The next time you get a thick plastic drinking straw, keep it. Rinse it out immediately.

2. When you get home, wash the straw thoroughly with detergent and water.

3. Cut the straw into varying lengths from 1" to 2" long to form Tubular Tubes. You're like, so done now.

Furball's Meow

Tubular tubes are soooo much fun on a smooth surface like the kitchen floor.

Put one on the floor and flick it with your finger. I love batting them around and aiming for under the fridge and stove. That's so hot.

difficulty level

time

5 minutes

play categories

stalk,
lazy cat

Tissue Kebab

Tissue Kebab's crunchy textures create layers of fun for both you and Kitty. It's also a great way to use up small scraps of tissue that aren't pristine enough to reuse as gift-wrap. Thankfully, the prep work for this kebab is fast and simple. No marinating required.

Although Tissue Kebab's not something to eat, for Kitty, it's a real treat!

What you'll need:

1 shoelace

Boxboard, such as cereal or cracker boxes

Scraps of tissue paper in any size, but they should be at least 2" x 2" in size.

Scissors

Furball's Meow

I like it when Mommy drags Tissue Kebab on the floor because I love the crinkly tissue sound.

When she whirls it over my head like a helicopter, I'll wrestle it down.

Now you have confirmation that Mommy is putting words in my mouth because what cat knows what a helicopter is?

1. Tie a double knot at one end of the shoelace to create a bulky knot.

2. Cut five circles out of the boxboard, approximately 2" in diameter. They don't need to be perfect circles, but the shapes should not have any sharp edges.

3. Fold a circle in half. Make a small cut midway on the folded end. See Figure 1.

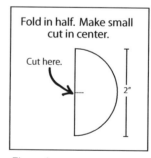

Figure 1

4. Open up the circle and fold it in half perpendicularly. Make another small cut so that you have a small "x" in the center. See Figure 2.

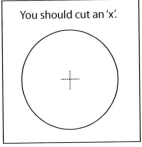

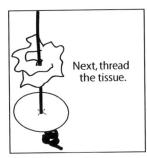

Figure 2

Figure 3

Figure 4

5. Thread the circle onto the shoelace and push it down until it sits on top of the knot. See Figure 3.

6. Take some tissue paper and loosely shape it into a 2" square. Gently poke a small hole in it and thread the shoelace through the tissue so that the tissue rests on top of the boxboard circle. See Figure 4.

7. Continue threading tissue loosely onto the kebab until you have about an inch of tissue in height. The tissue should be "puffy" and not compressed.

8. Repeat steps 3 to 6 until you have finished threading all five of the boxboard circles. Tissue Kebab is now ready to be sampled by Kitty's palate.

Fortune 8 Cat

Don't worry if Kitty rips Tissue Kebab to pieces. That's part of the fun. However, do be concerned if she tries to eat the tissue. That's a sure sign that tissue toys aren't suitable for your cat. You can always reuse the shoelace for another toy. Also, be sure to clean up any loose tissue scraps after playing.

difficulty level

time

2 minutes

play categories
stalk

Unwrap This!

Unwrap This! is one of those gifts that keeps on giving. Unfortunately (or fortunately from Kitty's perspective), many people are still over-wrapping presents with a plethora of tissue paper.

Before you recycle the pieces that are too crumpled to carefully fold and add to your very large stack of tissue paper to be reused, why not re-gift them to Kitty? Here's how...

What you'll need:

Used gift wrap tissue

Several of Kitty's favorite small toys

1. Remove tape, ribbon, bows or any other items that may be attached to the tissue.

2. Scatter two to four of Kitty's toys across the floor. Smooth out the tissue and place over the toys. Crunch a few balls of tissue and toss around the room. Stand back and watch Kitty Unwrap This!

Furball's Meow

Mommy makes Unwrap This! as a gift to keep me entertained. I love unwrapping the paper so much I don't leave a gift in return.

Fortune 8 Cat
Make sure that your cat doesn't like to eat paper and the toys you choose are safe. As well, don't leave Unwrap This! lying around if there's a risk of the humans in your house inadvertently stepping on hidden cat toys.

Just Say No to Excess Packaging

Hopefully in the future, you won't be able to make any of the toys in this section because wasteful packaging will become obsolete.

Start by observing the packaging in your life. Then, be creative on how to reduce it.

Alternatives to Throwaway Water Bottles

- Reusable containers made from BPA-free plastic
- SIGG reusable aluminum bottles
- Glass bottles
- Travel mugs
- Stainless steel water bottles

Share Your Ideas

Visit Furball's green website to share your creative ideas for reducing or reusing packaging.

www.greenlittlecat.com

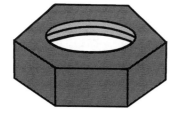

Ping Pong Pinball
The Shaker
The Fishing Pole
Houdini's Pendulum

Cat Toys Made Out of Household Items

Saturn Rings
Stringkey
Nuts 'n Bolts
Dream Cat-cher
Cat Beacon

play categories

chase

Ping Pong Pinball

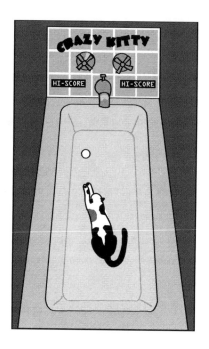

Ping Pong Pinball is more of a game than an actual toy. It only takes seconds to set up, but how many minutes (or hours) you and Kitty play is up to you, or more likely up to Kitty.

What you'll need:

1 ping pong ball or a soft lightweight ball less than 3/4" in diameter

1 clean and dry bathtub, with toiletries cleared out of the way and the stopper in the drain

1 hyper cat

Furball's Meow

This game may get a little crazy, so please be careful. If I get a little too excited I may swat you by accident.

1. Invite Kitty to the bathroom to play Ping Pong Pinball. Formal invitations are not necessary.

2. Take the ping pong ball and place it at one end of the tub.

3. With a flick of your arm, send the ball spinning around the tub like a ball on a roulette wheel.

4. Perform variations of the above maneuver as Kitty chases the ball around the tub.

5. The game is over when Kitty decides she is hungry. The winner is always Kitty.

The Shaker

The Shaker will inspire your Kitty to shake her booty like the old school dance hall days. All you need to do is shake the Shaker like a Polaroid picture. Then, roll it like a disco bowling ball down boogie alley.

When Kitty hears the first careless whispers of the Shaker's melodic rattle, she'll get into the groove faster than you can say, "Get on the dance floor."

What you'll need:

1 empty spool of thread, preferably less than 1.25" in diameter and less than 1.5" in height

Several grains of dried rice (uncooked)

Duct tape or masking tape

1. Tape the center hole of one end of the spool. Turn the spool over so that the open end is facing upwards.

2. Insert the dried grains of rice into the center hole until it is about 1/3 full.

3. Tape up the other end of the spool and get ready for Kitty to burn up the dance floor.

Furball's Meow

Mommy rolls the Shaker across the floor, but it never goes straight, making it so much more fun for me.

time

2 minutes

play categories

catch, chase,
stalk, wrestle,
lazy cat

The Fishing Pole

The Fishing Pole is ideal for a lazy Sunday afternoon. It's a multifunctional toy that can be used on its own or combined with Kitty's other toys to breathe new life into them. You can even resurrect that feather wand toy that Kitty gnawed down to a bald stump. Here's how...

What you'll need:

36" of hemp twine

1 elastic band, preferably at least 3/8" thick

1 stick at least 8" long – Some sticky ideas include a used clean chopstick, a "bald stump" wand toy that Kitty has torn the toy off of, or a wooden dowel.

1. Tie one end of the hemp twine around the elastic band. Double knot it to ensure that it's secure.

2. Take the elastic band and wrap it tightly around one end of your stick. If your stick tapers on one end, wrap the elastic band around the thicker end.

Furball's Meow

Get off the couch and come play with me! Ha ha, now I get to nap on the sofa.

3. Make a slip knot (see page 112 for instructions) on the other end of the twine. Secure one of Kitty's favorite toys through the loop and you're ready to start fishing.

Fortune 8 Cat

If you're using a wooden stick, be careful not to exert too much force on it. Wood is not as flexible as plastic, so too much force could cause the stick to splinter or break.

"When I play with my cat, how do I know that she is not passing time with me rather than I with her?"

- Michel de Montaigne

time

1 minute

play categories

catch, chase,
stalk, lazy cat

Houdini's Pendulum

No rabbit in that hat. Hello shiny ball!

Houdini was the master of escape, but Houdini's Pendulum won't pull a disappearing act on you. Although Kitty has a penchant for "accidentally" losing toys under the fridge (stove, sofa, crack behind the sofa, really hard to reach space behind the bed, etc.), she'll be hard pressed to make this toy vanish into thin air.

This interactive toy is a glittery ball on a string and you're the star performer of this show. Make the ball dance, bounce off walls and hide behind furniture to entice Kitty to leap to her feet for a standing ovation and call for a repeat performance.

What you'll need:

Aluminum foil

1 shoelace

Furball's Meow

Drag the ball along the floor and jerk it suddenly upwards. Also, let it rebound off the walls. The faster you move the ball, the more fun it is for me (and of course, it's all about me).

1. Tie a knot at the end of the shoelace.

2. Crumple the foil firmly around the knot so that the foil forms a tight ball and is firmly attached to the shoelace. It's time for your performance. Read Furball's Meow for a few star tips.

Fortune 8 Cat

It is really important to watch Kitty to make sure she doesn't try to eat the toy. Eating foil could result in her final disappearing act and we all know that even Houdini couldn't return from his last disappearance. If you think your cat may have a penchant to eat foil, stop all play and safely dispose of the toy.

Fortune 8 Cat felt it was important to include aluminum foil balls in this book because they are widely recommended as cat toys on the Internet, yet proper safety precautions are seldom mentioned. Please supervise your cat closely and if Kitty tries to eat it, the toy has got to beat it.

Did you know that aluminum foil made from 100% recycled aluminum is now widely available?

According to the manufacturer, recycled foil uses only 5% of the energy required to make regular foil.

Human Suggests

This is a great use for pieces of foil that are larger than the dish. Instead of over-wrapping the dish, simply tear off the excess foil and save it for making cat toys.

Furball's Meow

Give Saturn Rings a shake to catch my ear and I'll give chase as soon as it leaves your hand. Watch me run after it and swat it around the room.

Saturn Rings

Saturn Rings is shiny, light-weight and purrfectly sized for little cat paws. When it comes to intergalactic playtime, Kitty will discover that this toy is simply out of this world.

What you'll need:

Aluminum foil

1 jingle bell (optional), sal-vaged from a worn cat toy that you were going to throw out

1. Place the jingle bell in the center of the piece of foil. If you don't have a bell, you can skip this step.

2. Crumple the foil tightly to form a ball that is 1" in diameter. If you are using the jingle bell, it doesn't need to be exactly in the center. If it is a little askew, all the better for adding a slight warp to Saturn Rings' path. You've just manifested Saturn Rings into this universe.

Fortune 8 Cat

For foil toys, you should be extra vigilant in watching Kitty. Eating foil can be hazardous for your cat. Therefore, only give your cat these toys if you are 100% sure that they will play safely with them. Please supervise your cat closely and if in doubt, leave it out.

Stringkey

difficulty level

time

1 minute

play categories
stalk,
lazy cat

The key to Kitty's heart is a shiny object on a string. Stringkey is a great use for those spare keys that you've accumulated over the years and have no idea what they open.

Furball didn't like Stringkey, but his cousin Kiwi, loved it. Stringkey may just be the toy to unlock the playful kitten in your cat.

The key to my heart is tuna

What you'll need:

1 old house key

1 shoelace

1. Tie the shoelace to the key. Your Stringkey is now ready to unlock Kitty's heart. Try twittering the key under a light and dragging it along some soft carpet or hiding it behind the sofa. Kiwi loved Stringkey for practicing her stalking skills.

Fortune 8 Cat

Be very gentle when playing with Stringkey. Kitty wouldn't want to get hit in the head with a key.

Furball's Meow

I told Mommy not to put this toy in the book because I don't like it, but she insisted on it. I'll let her know my displeasure when I shred the first edition of the book.

Nuts 'n Bolts

Like many of the toys in this book, Nuts 'n Bolts was truly invented by Furball. One of his rattling mouse toys cracked open after being well loved (thrown down stairs, bounced off walls and gnawed on for hours).

When it cracked open, I discovered the secret to the rattling sound was a ball bearing and some plastic pegs. Although the gutted mouse no longer held any play appeal, Furball went berserk for the ball bearing.

Finally, a toy that was small and fast enough to be truly worthy of chasing. However, it soon became obvious to me that a ball bearing was not a safe toy. Ever try finding a ball bearing after it rolls down the hall? I substituted a metal nut instead. Furball went nuts for the nut and he bolted after it too.

Furball's Meow

Slide the nut across a smooth floor and it'll go really fast. So will I.

If your home has fancy floors, only play with this toy if you're sure the nut will not damage the floor. Otherwise, Nuts 'n Bolts is an incredibly fast, fun and easy cat toy. Here's how simple it can be...

What you'll need:

1 metal nut – It should be clean with no traces of rust or grease.

1. There's nuttin' to it. Just find a clean metal nut and slide it across the floor. Release the nut and Kitty will bolt after it.

Fortune 8 Cat

A safe play area is important. It should be enclosed and clutter-free so that you can find the nut easily. Don't forget to pick up the nut after playtime so that there's no chance someone could accidentally step on it or swallow it.

"The smallest feline is a masterpiece."
- Leonardo da Vinci

Dream Cat-cher

It's great when you can sell your old CDs for cash. However, if no one wants your Tom Jones album, here's a great use for it. Create a Dream "Cat-cher" that will transform an unwanted disc into the sweet harmonious sounds of a contented Kitty at play.

What you'll need:

Unwanted music CD, damaged or scratched is fine

Sunshine or a very bright, focused light source such as a halogen light

Human Suggests

Any type of disc will work for the Dream Catcher. You can also use unwanted DVDs or data CDs.

1. Hold the CD in the light so that it casts reflections throughout the room. Try angling the reflection so that Kitty can follow it along the floor and the walls. Your Dream Cat-cher is ready to fulfill Kitty's dreams of playing.

Furball's Meow

Please use your old Whitney Houston CD. When she hits the high notes, it scares me.

Fortune 8 Cat

Since playing with Kitty is always unpredictable, make sure to only use discs with music or computer files that you no longer want or need.

And, NEVER reflect the light into Kitty's eyes.

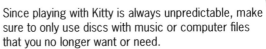

Cat Beacon

Just like Batman responding to the bat signal beamed onto a dark and ominous evening sky, Kitty will leap to action when she spots the Cat Beacon beckoning to her on your ceiling.

Shine it on your living room wall and watch Kitty fly around the room like a bat out of hell. You can be her superhero nemesis and send her on a wild chase to capture the villainous beam.

What you'll need:

1 watch with a reflective face

Sunlight

1. Position the watch face in a sunbeam so that it causes a reflection to appear on a wall at Kitty eye level, but be careful not to reflect the light in her eyes.

2. Practice moving the watch face to project the reflection across the room and ceiling. Wait for Kitty to spot and respond to the Cat Beacon.

Fortune 8 Cat
Don't reflect the light into Kitty's eyes. Arigato.

Furball's Meow
The reflection quivers like a moth and it's so much fun to chase.

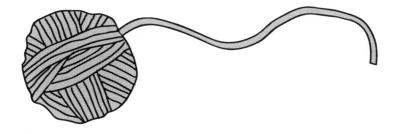

Spider Ballet

Hemp Hula

Utility Belt

Classic Ball of Yarn

Cat Toys Made from Craft Materials

Rapunzel's Braid

Whipper Snapper

Pharaoh's Pyramid

Jingles, the Reindeer

difficulty level

time

3 minutes

play categories

catch, wrestle,
lazy cat

Spider Ballet

A dancing daddy long legs might make you squeamish, but Spider Ballet's light steps and sweeping flutters will inspire Kitty to do her own pirouettes.

It only takes a couple of minutes to assemble Spider Ballet and once you do, you'll see that its twine legs are more like a poetic metaphor than a real replica of a spooky spider. After the first arachnid act, Kitty will be meowing for an encore.

What you'll need:

76" of hemp twine
(about 6.5 feet)

Scissors

1. Cut four pieces of twine that are 10" in length. These will form the spider's legs. You should also have a piece of twine leftover that is 36" in length.

2. Make a slip knot (see instructions on page 112) on the end of the 36" piece of twine.

Furball's Meow

Raise your arm above your head and swing Spider Ballet like a lasso. You'll look really funny to me and the whirring noise will make me want to join in the fun. Meow!

3. Then, line up the four 10" pieces and grasp them together. Fold them in half and pinch to bend them in the middle. Continue grasping them together. See Figure 1.

4. Feed the folded end through the slip knot so that it forms a loop. See Figure 2. For simplicity, the four lengths of twine are shown as a single black line in the illustration.

5. Thread the loose ends through the loop you formed in Step 4. See Figure 3. Pull tightly while also tightening the slip knot. The spider legs should now be secured to the 36" piece of twine. Spider Ballet is now finished and it's time to begin the opening act with Kitty in the starring role.

Human Suggests

Hemp twine can usually be purchased at a craft store or an earth-friendly product store. Be sure to buy the natural colored twine that is free of dyes.

Bend in half.

Figure 1

Feed through slip knot.

Figure 2

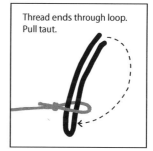

Thread ends through loop. Pull taut.

Figure 3

Hemp Hula

Kitty will think she's on a dream vacation when you make her the Hemp Hula. Let it soar over her head by throwing it just like you would a frisbee at the beach.

She'll catch it between her paws with elegant precision and maybe, just maybe, she'll bring it back to you to throw again. At the very least, you're guaranteed that she'll say, "Aloha!" every time you bring out this toy.

What you'll need:

1 piece of hemp twine, 19.5" in length

Scissors

1. Cut the twine into two pieces, one that is 12" in length and one that is 7.5" in length.

2. Fold the 12" piece in half and pinch it sharply at the halfway mark.

3. Tie the 12" piece tightly around the 7.5" piece, about 1.5" from one end. See Figure 1.

4. Then tie the 7.5" piece around the 12" piece to secure them together. You should now have three ends that are 6" in length, and a short end that is 1.5" in length.

Furball's Meow

Make me many. I can practice my frisbee catching skills when you toss the Hemp Hula in the air.

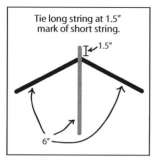

Tie long string at 1.5"
mark of short string.

1.5"

6"

Figure 1

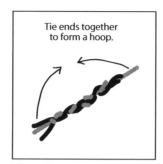

Tie ends together
to form a hoop.

Figure 2

5. Hold onto the short end and begin braiding the three 6" strings together.

6. Continue braiding until there is about 1.5" of string left unbraided.

7. To finish off the braid, tie two of the loose ends together. Then tie one of these ends to the third loose end. Ensure the knots are pulled tightly together.

8. You will now have a braided rope where there is a loose string on one end and three on the other end. See Figure 2. Take the single string and tie it to any of the loose ends on the other side. Make a double knot to secure it. You've just created a paw-sized Hemp Hula that's the perfect size for Kitty to flick with her paw.

Utility Belt

Give Kitty the Utility Belt and she'll strut around like a man in a shop full of shiny power tools. This multifunctional toy slices, dices and takes out the trash. The only thing it doesn't do is mow the lawn.

Ok, maybe it doesn't really do any of these things, but the basic model is a great toy and you can also upgrade it by attaching other toys. The Utility Belt will be Kitty's favorite do-it-yourself home amusement project.

Now that's what I call home improvement.

What you'll need:

3 pieces of hemp twine of equal length, approximately 3 to 4 feet long – To determine the best length, stand up with your arms to your sides and dangle the hemp twine. Add 12" to the length where it touches the floor.

1. Line up the three pieces of twine. Grasp them together and tie a double knot on one end as if they were one rope.

2. Braid the three pieces of twine together until you have about 3" remaining on the end.

3. Tie the ends in a knot to finish off the braid.

4. Make a slip knot at one end (see page 112 for directions). It's now time to reveal this new toy to Kitty.

Human Suggests

Attach the Firecracker (page 96) to the sturdy Utility Belt to create the ultimate power toy.

Furball's Meow

Mommy dangles the Utility Belt over my head and I can't resist swatting at it. When she attaches one of my toys, it's wrestling time.

Classic Ball of Yarn

When I was a kitten, we didn't have these fancy catnip toys. All I had to chase was a ball of yarn.

This is the quintessential classic of homemade cat toys. Since the early days of woolly mitts and itchy hats, generations of kittens have enjoyed the simple pleasure of chasing a ball of yarn.

This is a great use for those leftover remnants of yarn, and you can combine remnants until the ball is the perfect size for your Kitty.

What you'll need:

Leftover ends of yarn

1. Begin winding one end of the yarn upon itself.

2. Continue winding the yarn tightly to shape a ball that is about 1" in diameter.

Fortune 8 Cat

Keep an eye on Kitty to make sure that she's not the type to eat yarn. If she is, take the yarn away from her and don't give her toys made with string. If ingested, long string can twist in Kitty's intestines and we don't want that to happen.

When playtime is over, put the yarn away so that the humans don't trip over the yarn. Be kind, rewind.

Furball's Meow

No special instructions here. Just give me the ball and my cat instincts will know what to do next.

difficulty level

time

45-60 minutes

play categories
catch, wrestle,
lazy cat

Rapunzel's Braid

Kitty:

"Rapunzel, Rapunzel, let down your long braided hair so that I may rip it to shreds in a game of tug-of-war."

Rapunzel:

"No freaking way!!!"

Understandably, this fair maiden isn't keen on the idea about having a furry ball of claws and teeth dangling from her long hair, even though you've probably experienced it.

However, you can make Kitty her own Rapunzel's Braid in under an hour which is much less time than it would take for you to grow a braid.

What you'll need:

Yarn of average thickness – This is a great use of leftover yarn ends.

1 pair of medium to large sized knitting needles

Furball's Meow

This braid is the best thing for tug of war. Meow!

1. Cast on two stitches and leave about 3" of yarn hanging at the end.

2. Knit one row. Purl one row. Continue alternating the stitches until the strand is about 18" long. Finish it off and also leave 3" of loose yarn at the other end.

3. Repeat steps 1 and 2 to produce two more 18" strands.

4. You now have three 18" strands. Line them up and tie them together using the 3" loose yarn at the ends.

5. Then, proceed to braid the strands together.

6. When you have finished braiding them together, complete Rapunzel's Braid by tying the loose ends together. You're ready to let some hair down and engage Kitty in some hair-raising fun.

"Cat lovers can readily be identified. Their clothes always look old and well used. Their sheets look like bath towels, and their bath towels look like a collection of knitting mistakes."
- Eric Gurney

difficulty level

time

45-60 minutes

play categories

catch, wrestle,
lazy cat

Whipper Snapper

If your Kitty is lucky enough to have a "Grandma" who knits, then your young whipper snapper grandcat can plead to Granny to make her a Whipper Snapper. If Granny's a quilter and not a knitter, then it's up to you to deliver the goods.

Fortunately for you, Kitty's not picky about how the finished product looks, so anyone with the most elementary knitting skills can whip up a Whipper Snapper.

Purr, is that angora?

What you'll need:

Yarn of average thickness – This is a great use for left-over yarn ends.

1 pair of medium to large sized knitting needles

Furball's Meow

When I'm lying on my back, Mommy tickles my tummy with the Whipper Snapper. It makes me squiggle and makes her giggle, and I always snag it between my paws. It's so delightfully fun.

1. Begin by casting on six stitches.

2. Knit one row. Purl the next row.

3. Repeat step 2 until the Whipper Snapper is about 4" long.

4. Then knit two rows. Resume alternating between purling one row and knitting the other. By switching the stitches, you'll create the "handle" for the Whipper Snapper.

5. Continue to knit one row and purl the other until the Whipper Snapper is between 16" to 20" long, including the handle. Finish off the stitching. Now, it's time to whip Kitty up into a playing frenzy.

Pharaoh's Pyramid

Cats were originally desert creatures that were revered in ancient Egypt. Pay homage to Kitty's heritage and the brilliant Egyptian architects with the mythical Pharaoh's Pyramid.

This three-sided pyramid is sturdy, yet lightweight, and it also possesses the ability to mesmerize Kitty. The next time Kitty demands to be worshipped, present her with this architectural marvel so that she can reconnect with her royal lineage.

What you'll need:

1 pipe cleaner – Usually when people buy pipe cleaners, they end up having dozens leftover that sit in a box in the closet. Cat toys are a great idea for using them. If you don't already have pipe cleaners handy, ask friends and family if they have some.

Continued on next page...

Pharaoh's Pyramid continued

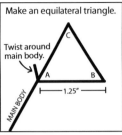

Make an equilateral triangle.

Twist around main body.

1.25"

Figure 1

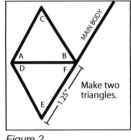

Make two triangles.

MAIN BODY

Figure 2

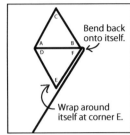

Bend back onto itself.

Wrap around itself at corner E.

Figure 3

1. Fold over 1/4" of the pipe cleaner at one end. Press it tightly flat against the rest of the pipe cleaner so that the sharp point is bent inwards and does not protrude. Repeat with the other end.

2. Starting from one end, bend the pipe cleaner to make a 1.25"" equilateral triangle. To do this, first bend 1/4" at a right angle. Then, measure and bend the pipe cleaner at 1.25". Measure and bend another 1.25". Form the triangle and twist the 1/4" end around the main body of the pipe cleaner to secure the triangle. See Figure 1.

3. You will now create a second triangle that shares one side with the original triangle (Side A to B). Measure and bend 1.25". Repeat. Join this to the original triangle by wrapping the end once through Corner B. See Figure 2.

4. Fold the pipe cleaner so that it traces Side E to F of the second triangle. Wrap the end through Corner E of the original triangle. See Figure 3.

Furball's Meow

Now that you are aware of the regal heritage of cats, perhaps you had better acquiesce to our every whim. Oh yeah, you already do that.

5. Fold the two triangles towards each other until Corner C is about 1.25" away from Corner E. See Figure 4.

6. With the remaining end of the pipe cleaner, bend it towards Corner C. At 1.25", secure it to Corner C. See Figure 5.

7. Twist the remaining pipe cleaner around any side of the pyramid so that there are no sharp ends poking out. You have just created the Pharaoh's Pyramid in minutes as compared to years for the Great Pyramid of Giza. Give yourself a pat on the back.

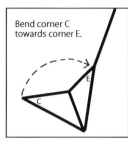

Bend corner C towards corner E.

Figure 4

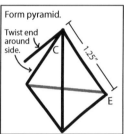

Form pyramid.

Twist end around side.

1.25"

Figure 5

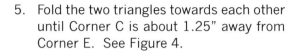

Human Suggests

Don't worry if it's not a perfect pyramid. As long as you twist together some sort of 3D form, you've added your own brilliance to the Pharaoh's Pyramid.

Fortune 8 Cat

Before playing, double-check to make sure there are no sharp ends.

"I have an Egyptian cat. He leaves a pyramid in every room"
- Rodney Dangerfield

Jingles, the Reindeer

Ring in the holidays with the merry sound of Jingles, the Reindeer.

Because this toy is so quick and easy to make, it's a purrfect (this bad pun is used in every cat book, why should this book be different?) gift for Kitty.

You can make it any time of the year as Kitty will certainly be in festive spirits when there's a new toy.

What you'll need:

1 pipe cleaner – See page 77 for sources of pipe cleaners.

1 mid-sized jingle bell (approximately 1/2" to 3/4" in diameter), repurposed from an old cat toy that you were going to throw away

1 pencil or pen

1. Fold over 1/4" of the pipe cleaner at one end. Press it tightly flat against the rest of the pipe cleaner so that the sharp point is bent inwards and does not protrude. Repeat with the other end.

2. Thread the bell onto the pipe cleaner until it reaches the midway point.

Furball's Meow

Give Jingles a shake and I'll perk up my ears when I hear the ringing bell. Toss the toy into the air and I'll be the one flying like one of Santa's reindeer.

3. Bend the pipe cleaner to form a ring about 1" in diameter at the mid-point. Twist the ends together to secure the circle. See Figure 1.

4. Wrap each end of the pipe cleaner around the pencil or pen to form a spiral coil. See Figure 2. Jingles, the Reindeer is now ready to bring some joy into the festive season.

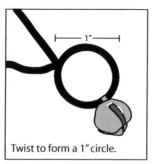

Twist to form a 1" circle.

Figure 1

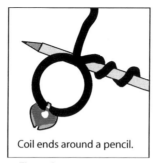

Coil ends around a pencil.

Figure 2

Fortune 8 Cat
Before playing, double-check to make sure there are no sharp ends.

"The cat has too much spirit to have no heart."

- Ernest Menaul

Kitty Kat
Number One Mouser

ABC Cats Inc.
123 Cat Alley
Los Gatos, CA 99999
1-800-CAT-CALL

Cat Toys Made Using Office and School Items

Biz Card Flicker

ID Badge

Penned Up Energy

Cerlox Holmes

Kitty Broomstick

Biz Card Flicker

"Watashi no meishi desu" (Here is my business card) is one of the first phrases I learned in Japanese 101. With solemn formality, the students would practice uttering this phrase and handing over their business cards, respectfully offered with two hands.

Here in North America, the process is definitely much more casual and people are less particular about who they give their cards too. Maybe they're thinking they ordered a box of 500 and need to get rid of them before they change jobs.

As a result, I'm sure, like me, you must have collected a pile of business cards from people you don't even remember. Before you chuck "John Doe, Sales Manager of ABC Company" into the circular filing system, why not introduce this fine gentleman to Kitty? She'll be pleased to make his acquaintance in the form of the Biz Card Flicker. And this time, he'll leave a lasting impression.

What you'll need:

1 standard sized business card

1. Pleat the business card lengthwise in an accordion style. Each pleat should be about 1/4" thick. You should have about five to six folds in total. See Figure 1.

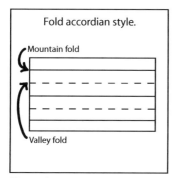

Figure 1

2. Fold the pleated business card in half to form a fan. Press firmly so that the fold stays in place. The Biz Card Flicker is now ready to meet Kitty.

"The ideal of calm exists in a sitting cat."
- Jules Reynard

Furball's Meow

Mommy makes the most delicious sound by running her fingernail on the folds. Sometimes she also brushes this toy on the carpet. I can't wait until she flicks the Biz Card Flicker across the room for me to chase.

play categories

catch, stalk,
lazy cat

ID Badge

Slay the demons of a lousy job by letting Kitty have her way with your old identification badge.

In no time at all, that company logo will be scratched away, even if it's a garish royal purple or a blinding neon red. Let the healing begin!

Cubicled cat ready to shred.

If you don't have an old ID badge, ask your cubicled friends if they have one. If you tell them what you intend to do with their old badges, you'll be amazed at how many donors will appear.

As tempting as it may be on certain days, DON'T use your current company badge. Kitty could do some serious damage to it. You might have to pay to replace it or worse yet, you won't be able to get into the office! If work is that bad, you can always start looking for a new job such as writing books about niche topics.

You can also substitute any other plastic card such as an expired gift card, or those annoying "fake credit cards" that you get in the mail to entice you to apply for one.

Furball's Meow

It's all fun and games to me, but if Mommy says it's therapeutic, then that's pawsome!

What you'll need:

1 plastic ID badge that you no longer need, or an expired gift card

1 shoelace

1 large paperclip, approximately 1.75" in length

1 hole puncher

Human Suggests

Any resemblance to a corporation, living or dead, is purely coincidental. No actual ID badges were harmed in the making of this toy.

1. If you're using a gift card or if your ID badge doesn't have a hole in it, punch a hole on one end of the plastic card. See Figure 1.

2. Thread the paperclip through the hole so that the card is hooked onto the paperclip like a key on a key ring.

3. Next, pass the end of the shoelace through the other end of the paperclip. Tie the two ends of the shoelace together in a double knot. The ID Badge is now ready to show you why cats are so great for relieving stress.

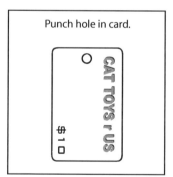

Figure 1

Did you know it's easy to opt out of pre-screened credit offers? While you'll lose a source of materials for cat toys, it's much better to reduce this waste of paper.

Visit **www.optoutprescreen.com** for details.

Penned Up Energy

Whether you're an accomplished author penning the next Great Gatsby, a humble poet composing an ode to the feline, or simply someone writing a cat toy book, you can't help but notice that Kitty will perch herself nearby and be intensely fascinated as you write.

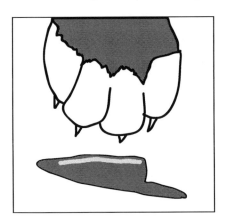

The twitchy movements of your pen and the soft rustling sounds of the ballpoint tip scratching the paper are irresistible to her. So how do you continue writing without interruption? Simply use what you have in hand to help Kitty release her "penned up" energy.

What you'll need:

Pen with a separate cap

1. Place the cap on the pen to cover up the ink. Gently tap Kitty's paw, which will entice her to try trapping the pen with her paw.

2. After her interest is piqued, remove the pen cap and slide it across a smooth floor such as hardwood or tiles. She'll use up her pent up energy to chase the cap.

Fortune 8 Cat
Use a pen that has run out of ink to minimize the risk of any accidents.

Furball's Meow

If you spin the pen on the floor, I'll chase that too. It's irresistible.

Cerlox Holmes

Finally, there's a fun use for old reports and dusty school projects. The game is afoot with Cerlox Holmes. It's elementary, my dear cat lover. Simply remove the cerlox binding from your old reports, recycle the paper and follow these instructions to send Kitty on a wild chase.

Cerlox binding is also known as comb binding. Ideal sources include old training manuals from work, that business plan you wrote for marketing class or handouts from seminars. Just make sure you don't need the information anymore.

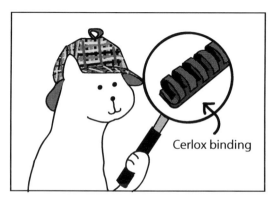

Cerlox binding

What you'll need:

Cerlox bound document

Scissors

1. Carefully remove the cerlox binding from the report. Don't forget to recycle the paper.

2. Cut the cerlox binding into pieces, ranging from three to five links or about 1.5" to 3" in length. Cerlox Holmes is now ready for Kitty's investigation.

Furball's Meow

Squeeze Cerlox Holmes to make a tantalizing "click click" noise that I'll want to investigate straight away. Whip it across a smooth floor and I'll be on the chase.

Kitty Broomstick

Who says that only witches and Harry Potter have all the fun when it comes to flying broomsticks? Your Kitty can have her own deluxe broom in a matter of minutes with minimal effort on your part.

Since Kitty already knows how to fly through the air, the Kitty Broomstick will actually help keep her grounded. In this case however, being grounded is a cackle of fun.

What you'll need:

1 sheet of paper, 8.5" x 11" in size – Junk mail letters are fantastic for this.

Scissors

Furball's Meow

Close a door with me on one side and you on the other. Wiggle the broom under the crack and I'll pounce on it every time.

The Kitty Broomstick is also a great toy to use with the Peek-a-boo House (page 28).

1. Fold the paper into thirds. See Figure 1.

2. Using the scissors, make 2" cuts approximately 1/4" to 1/3" wide on one end of the paper. See Figure 2.

3. Start rolling the paper lengthwise, starting with a width that is about 1/3" to 3/8" wide. See Figure 3.

4. When you have finished rolling, press the paper flat. Kitty's Broomstick is now ready for some flying fun.

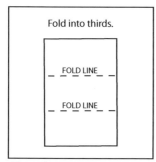

Figure 1

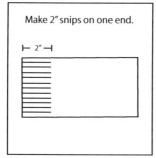

Figure 2

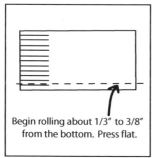

Figure 3

Fortune 8 Cat

If you're going to wiggle the broom under a door, it's best to do this on a tiled floor so that Kitty's claws will not damage the floor's surface. This is not a good game to play on carpet, as Kitty won't hesitate to tear up the carpet with her claws.

Did you know you can reduce your junk mail by requesting to have your name removed from mailing lists through the Direct Marketing Association?

To learn how, visit their consumer information site at **www.dmachoice.org.**

Catnip Satchel 101
Firecracker
Beanbag Ravioli
Wrestle Sausage

Cat Toys Made from Old Clothing

Lazy Wrestle Sausage
Ratty Sock on a String
Go Fish
Polar Ribbon
Catnip Bowtie

time

20-30 minutes

play categories
catch, chase,
wrestle

Catnip Satchel 101

The Catnip Satchel is one of those basic toys that every cat household should have. It's easy to make and even faster if you have a sewing machine. Plus, you can recycle your old clothes into an endless supply of eco-friendly toys for Kitty.

What you'll need:

Old shirt made from a medium-weight fabric

Stuffing material such as batting or fabric scraps

Dried catnip, preferably organic

Needle and thread or a threaded sewing machine

Scissors

1. Cut a 6" x 7" rectangle out of your old shirt.

2. Fold the rectangle in half crosswise, right sides of the fabric together. See Figure 1.

3. Beginning at the folded edge, sew two sides of the rectangle together as shown in Figure 2. Leave a 1/4" seam allowance.

4. If you are sewing with a needle and thread, reinforce the seam by sewing back in the other direction, with the new seam positioned just inside the first line of stitching. If you are using a sewing machine, don't forget to backstitch at the beginning and end points.

Furball's Meow

I love toys made out of your old clothes, especially if they still smell like you.

5. Turn the rectangle inside out.

6. Fill with batting or fabric scraps while liberally mixing in two to four tablespoons of the dried catnip. Pack the satchel so that it is loose, but not too firm.

7. Tuck the fabric at the open end inside. Using the needle and thread, sew the opening shut and stitch over it again to reinforce the seam. You've just completed one of the most classic and beloved cat toys.

Human Suggests

If your Kitty doesn't go crazy for catnip, I would recommend that you try Beanbag Ravioli (page 98) or the Wrestle Sausage (page 101) instead.

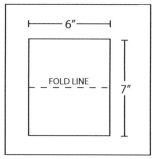

Figure 1

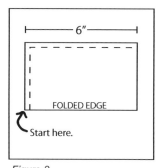

Figure 2

Times have changed since our moms made us stuffed pillows. The ubiquitous cotton batting now comes in organic cotton and a bamboo/cotton blend.

Fortune 8 Cat

If you're using batting, check the toy regularly for signs of wear. If the stuffing starts to come out, remember the Safety Commandment, "If it falls apart, toss and restart."

When using old clothes, always check to make sure the fabric is colorfast. If the dye comes off, the material is not suitable for cat toys.

Firecracker

It might not be the 4th of July, but when you detonate this Firecracker, Kitty will put on a colorful show that will rival any fireworks finale. Watch her explosive reactions as she wrestles down this Firecracker, stopping only when she has fully extinguished it. Let the fireworks begin!

What you'll need:

1 old long-sleeve shirt or top

Pinch of organic catnip (and a pinch of love)

Scissors

1. Cut the sleeves from the shirt. See Figure 1.

2. Cut the midsection of the shirt into fabric scraps about 3" x 2" in size (they do not need to be exact). You will need enough scraps to loosely stuff about one third of a sleeve.

3. Take one sleeve and loosely stuff the middle third with the fabric scraps. Add in the pinch of catnip. See Figure 2.

Furball's Meow

I like it when Mommy lights up the Firecracker. She ties the Utility Belt (page 72) on one end and then we play tug of war.

Thanks Uncle Austin for this great toy idea.

Cut sleeves off.

Figure 1

Stuff middle third of one sleeve with catnip and scraps.

Stuff

Figure 2

4. Fold the ends of the sleeve over like you are wrapping a package. Set aside. See Figure 3.

5. Take the other sleeve and tie one end tightly onto itself to create a long tube-like pouch. See Figure 4.

6. Take the stuffed sleeve you set aside and insert it into the pouch formed by the other sleeve. See Figure 5. Be sure to leave enough fabric at the open end of the sleeve so that you can tie it off.

7. Finish the toy by knotting the open end of the sleeve tightly closed. The Firecracker is now ready to light a fire under Kitty.

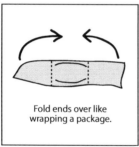

Fold ends over like wrapping a package.

Figure 3

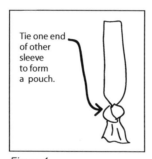

Tie one end of other sleeve to form a pouch.

Figure 4

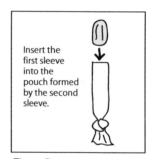

Insert the first sleeve into the pouch formed by the second sleeve.

Figure 5

Fortune 8 Cat
When using old clothes, remember to test the fabric for colorfastness.

Beanbag Ravioli

Beanbag Ravioli is a favorite on Kitty's menu. It's a delectable morsel that is best served tossed to Kitty. While it does take a little bit of extra effort, the most satisfying meals are those made with heart. Once she gets a taste of Beanbag Ravioli, Kitty will be sending her compliments to the chef!

What you'll need:

3" x 6" rectangle of scrap fabric – A woven weave is better to work with than stretchy material. An old button-down shirt is ideal.

Approximately 1 to 2 Tbsp of dried lentils

Pinch of catnip, to taste

Threaded sewing machine – You can also sew this by hand, but it will take more time and be less sturdy.

Needle and thread

Pinking shears or scissors

1. Using the scissors, cut the fabric into two 3" x 3" squares.

2. Place the fabric squares together with the right sides facing OUT.

3. Leaving a 3/8" seam allowance, use the sewing machine (or needle and thread if you are doing it by hand), to sew three sides of the squares together. Be sure to start 3/8" from the edge on the first side and pause 3/8" from the edge on the third side. Don't forget to back stitch when you first get started. See Figure 1.

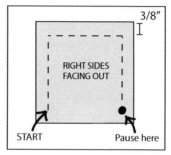

Figure 1

4. If you're using a sewing machine, make sure that the needle is still piercing the fabric on the last stitch. Lift up the pressure foot, leaving the needle in the down position to anchor the fabric. The three sewn sides now form a pocket. It's time to stuff your ravioli. Carefully insert the dried lentils and the catnip into the pocket until you are satisfied with the "beanbag feel." The pocket should not be over-stuffed. See Figure 2.

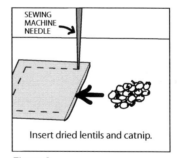

Figure 2

Continued on next page...

Beanbag Ravioli continued

5. Sew the open end shut. If you're using a sewing machine, push the lentils and catnip out of the way of the pressure foot. Replace the pressure foot in the down position and sew the side of the square shut. Finish by backstitching and cutting the loose threads.

6. Use the pinking shears to trim just enough of the edge to give the ravioli a zigzag finish to minimize fraying of the fabric. Try not to cut too closely to the seam. See Figure 3. Beanbag Ravioli is now ready to be served.

Figure 3

Furball's Meow

Give the Ravioli a shake and crinkle and I'll come running like it's chow time.

Fortune 8 Cat

Keep Beanbag Ravioli dry to prevent the lentils from getting ripe in a bad way. Take the toy away if Kitty tries to eat it. If you don't have pinking shears, it's okay to leave the edges unfinished, but they may begin to fray sooner. As with all toys, if it starts to fall apart, it's time to throw it away.

P.S. Don't forget to test the fabric for colorfastness.

Wrestle Sausage

Wrestle Sausage, as its name implies, is for cats who love to wrestle. It's the size of a small rodent, but it makes a Kitty-satisfying crinkly crackle sound when she attacks it. As an added bonus, Wrestle Sausage does not leave a bloody mess on your doorstep.

Ideally, you should make Wrestle Sausage from one of your old T-shirts so that Kitty can enjoy that lived-in smell, giving Wrestle Sausage the added "scents" of realism. Soft jersey cotton is also an excellent texture for Kitty to sink her claws into. And, you'll have fun recycling your T-shirt into something other than a garage rag.

What you'll need:

Old cotton T-shirt

1 crunchy plastic bag, grocery store style

1 Tbsp organic catnip (optional)

1 sturdy shoelace or the Utility Belt (page 72)

Needle and thread

Scissors

Chopstick or pencil

Threaded sewing machine (optional)

Continued on next page...

Wrestle Sausage continued

1. Cut two 9" x 5" rectangles from the old T-shirt.

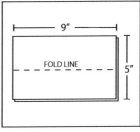

Figure 1

2. Place the rectangles one on top of the other. The material is being doubled up for durability. Fold in half lengthwise. See Figure 1.

3. Using either a needle and thread or a sewing machine, stitch the rectangles together. Start from the folded end on the short side and continue down the long side, leaving a 3/8" seam allowance. When you reach the end of the long side, finish off the stitching if you are using a sewing machine. If you are sewing by hand, go back and sew a reinforcing seam along the inside of the first line of stitching. See Figure 2.

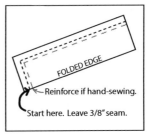

Figure 2

4. Turn the sausage inside out. Use a chopstick or pencil to help you. See Figure 3.

5. Cut a 7.5" wide section from the plastic bag lengthwise. See Figure 4.

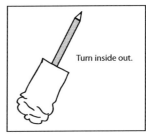

Figure 3

Furball's Meow

I loved the Wrestle Sausage so much, I played with the same one until it fell apart and then Mommy took it away. Luckily, she made two at the same time and had a replacement ready on hand.

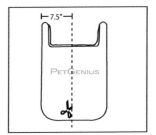

Figure 4

Figure 5

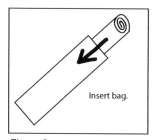

Figure 6

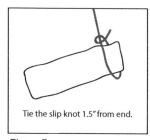

Tie the slip knot 1.5" from end.

Figure 7

6. Lay the section of plastic bag flat and sprinkle catnip evenly across its surface. Begin loosely rolling the bag so that it will be the right width to fit inside the sausage. See Figure 5.

7. Insert the rolled up plastic bag into the sausage. See Figure 6.

8. Tuck in the unfinished ends at the open side of the sausage. Use the needle and thread to sew it closed.

9. Tie a slip knot in the shoelace or Utility Belt. See page 112 for instructions on tying a slip knot. Secure the loop over the Wrestle Sausage about 1.5" from the end. Now you're ready to wrestle with Kitty from a safe distance.

Fortune 8 Cat
When using old clothes, always check the fabric for colorfastness.

Human Suggests

Use fun colors and patterns to sew homemade gifts for the cat lovers in your life.

Lazy Wrestle Sausage

There are times when Kitty wants to wrestle and there are times when your socks get holes in them. Do you see the synergy and the interconnectedness? A butterfly beats its wings in China and Kitty gets a new toy.

As the name implies, this is the slacker version of the Wrestle Sausage. Think of the Wrestle Sausage as haute couture and the Lazy Wrestle Sausage as a copycat. However, if you decide to use your Prada socks, then who can really say which is high fashion?

Regardless, there will be rare moments when you won't feel like sewing for 30 minutes to make Kitty toys on demand. Luckily, Kitty will enjoy Lazy Wrestle Sausage just as much as the non-lazy version.

What you'll need:

1 old sock, patchy and thinning is fine

1 crunchy plastic bag, grocery store style

1 Tbsp organic catnip (optional)

1 sturdy shoelace or the Utility Belt (page 72)

Scissors

Furball's Meow

Wear the socks before we play. I want to smell your feet when I dig my claws in and chomp down on this toy.

1. Put the catnip in the sock.

2. Stuff the sock with the plastic bag. It should feel soft and pliable to the touch. If it feels too stiff, cut away excess plastic from the bag until you achieve the desired texture.

3. Tie a slip knot in the shoelace or Utility Belt. See page 112 for instructions on how to tie one. Insert 2" of the open end of the sock through the noose and then pull the knot tight. The Lazy Wrestle Sausage is now ready.

Human Suggests:

Wash the sock first and then wear it around the house for an hour or two to get eau de foot.

"There are two means of refuge from the miseries of life: music and cats."

- Albert Schweitzer

difficulty level

time

1 minute

play categories

catch, stalk,
wrestle, lazy cat

Ratty Sock on a String

The name says it all...

Furball's Meow

Mommy drags the sock along the edge of the floor so that I can pretend it's a scurrying mouse. Sometimes she also makes the sock jump up in the air and I'll fly up after it.

Don't tell her, but I pretend not to notice the difference between this sock and her good socks, especially if she's wearing them.

What you'll need:

1 shoelace

1 old ratty sock

1. Tie a slip knot at the end of the shoelace. See page 112 for instructions on how to tie one.

2. Insert one end of the old ratty sock through the noose and pull it tight. You are now ready to play with your Ratty Sock on a String.

Go Fish

difficulty level

time

1 minute

play categories

catch, wrestle,
lazy cat

It's time to go fishing and Kitty is what you're trying to catch. The lure is Go Fish and this bait is so enticing, Kitty will hook her claws in and not want to let go. It takes less than a minute to set the bait and you'll reel Kitty in with this fun and interactive toy.

What you'll need:

1 old shoelace

1. Tie a knot at the end of the string. You're done. Now, go fish.

Furball's Meow

Mommy thinks this is ridiculously simple and wonders how I could possibly find it fun.

She just doesn't understand that when she dangles Go Fish in front of me, the little twitching knot reminds me of all the small creatures that I love to chase.

difficulty level

time

5 minutes

play categories

catch, wrestle,
lazy cat

Polar Ribbon

The Polar Ribbon isn't made from wrapping ribbon. Instead, it repurposes your linty, pilly, worn out polar fleece jacket.

You can swirl the Polar Ribbon in the air and watch Kitty execute a floor routine like an Olympic gymnast. And, even though Kitty's the one doing the acrobatics, you'll be the one scoring a perfect "10" for making her this fun and interactive toy.

Furball's Meow

Twirl and swirl the ribbon above my head to encourage me to jump. When I'm feeling lazy and lying on my side, you can also dangle the Polar Ribbon above my belly. I can't resist swatting at it.

What you'll need:

Old polar fleece jacket or top – If the top is still good to wear, by all means donate it. However, if it's really pathetic looking, then it's perfect cat toy fodder.

1 clean, used chopstick

Thick rubber band, like the ones used for broccoli

Scissors

1. Cut a 1" wide lengthwise strip from the polar fleece top. Continue cutting strips until the strips add up to 50" to 70" in length. For the average adult-sized jacket, you will probably need to cut two strips. See Figure 1.

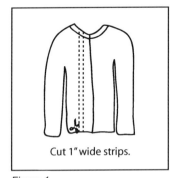

Cut 1" wide strips.

Figure 1

2. Tie the strips together with double knots to form a very long ribbon.

3. Tie a knot at one end of the ribbon. This will provide something for Kitty to grab onto with her claws.

4. Tie the other end of the ribbon around the elastic band.

5. Wrap the elastic band around the wide end of the chopstick until it is secure. See Figure 2. The Polar Ribbon is now ready for Kitty to begin her gymnastics routine.

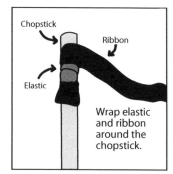

Figure 2

Fortune 8 Cat

When using old clothes, always check the fabric for colorfastness. Also be careful not to exert too much force on the chopstick. Wood is not as flexible as plastic, so too much force could cause it to splinter or break.

Carry a pair of travel chopsticks with you or leave a pair in your desk at work. With the growing concern over the impact of disposable chopsticks, there are now more design options than ever before.

You can choose from portable chopstick cases, reusable organic bamboo chopsticks and collapsible stainless steel ones.

difficulty level

time

3 minutes

play categories

catch, chase,
wrestle

Catnip Bowtie

Kitty is always dressed to the nines for all of her nine lives. She's also simply stunning "au naturel" which is why the Catnip Bowtie isn't for her to wear. It is however, featured prominently in this season's ready-to-play collection and will send Kitty chasing down the runway.

What you'll need:

Old polar fleece jacket or top

1 Tbsp organic catnip

Scissors

So this is why it's called a catwalk.

1. Cut a 16" x 3" rectangle from the fabric. Lay it flat.

2. Place the tablespoon of catnip in the center of the fabric. Be sure to leave at least 1" on either side. See Figure 1.

3. Fold the fabric in half lengthwise. See Figure 2. Then fold it again. See Figure 3. It will resemble a long tube.

4. While pinching the ends of the tube around the catnip to keep it from spilling out, tie the tube into a tight knot. See Figure 4.

5. Double knot the tube. The Catnip Bowtie is now ready for the discerning Kitty fashionista.

Furball's Meow

Before Mommy puts the catnip in the Bowtie, she rubs it between her fingers. She says she learned on a cooking show that this releases the aroma of the herbs. It also makes her fingers smell yummy.

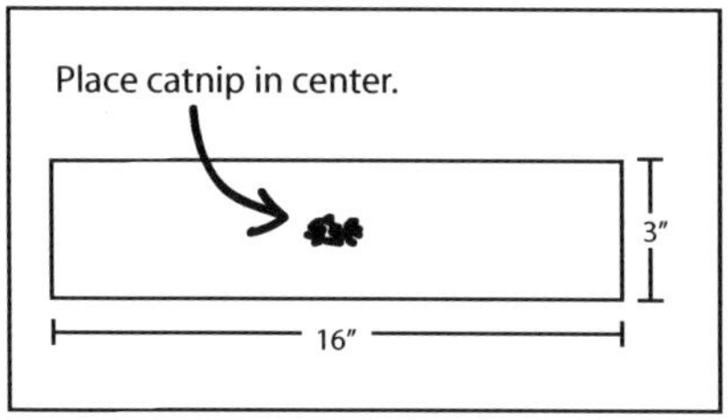

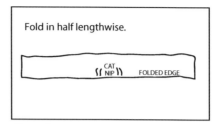

Place catnip in center.

3"

16"

Figure 1

Fold in half lengthwise.

CAT NIP   FOLDED EDGE

Figure 2

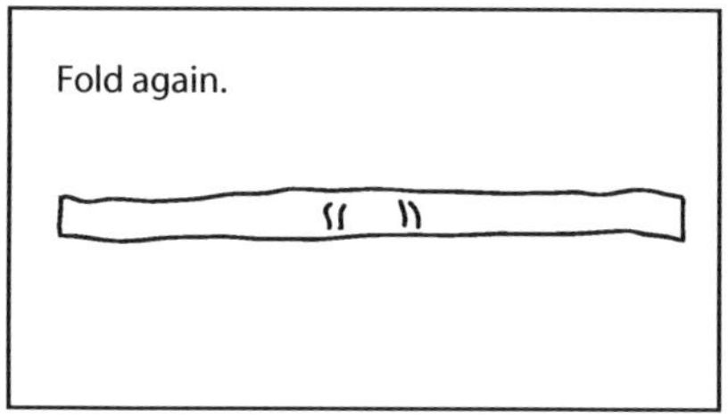

Fold again.

Figure 3

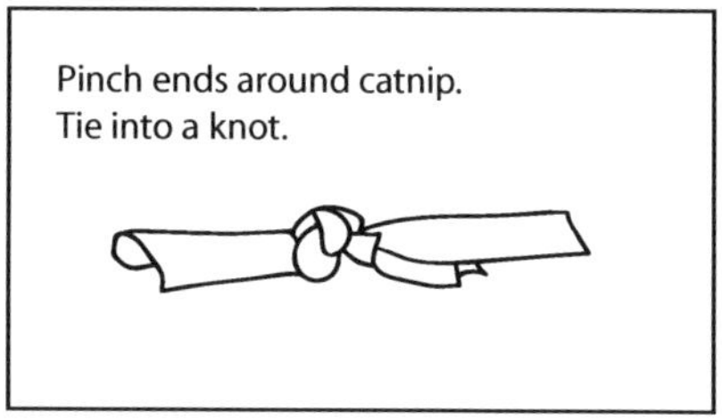

Pinch ends around catnip.
Tie into a knot.

Figure 4

Fortune 8 Cat

When using old clothes, always check the fabric for colorfastness. Kitty would not appreciate dye coming off on her.

How to Tie a Slip Knot

A slip knot, also known as a running knot, is an essential element for making your own cat toys. It enables you to securely attach a cat toy to a string, yet also remove the toy with ease. Need I say more?

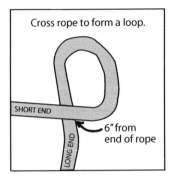

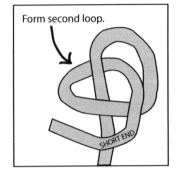

Step 1

To begin making a slip knot, cross one end of the rope over itself about 6" from the end of the rope. This will form a loop in the shape of the letter P.

Step 2

Take the short end of the rope and feed it through the loop you just created in Step 1. Continue pulling the short end of the rope loosely through the loop in a downwards direction.

Step 3

Start curving the short end of the rope upwards. This will form a second loop to the left of the first loop as illustrated above.

Feed end through second loop.

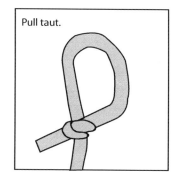

Pull taut.

Step 4

Feed the short end of the rope upwards through the second loop that was formed in Step 3.

Step 5

Pull the short end taut so that you knot the rope onto itself. The knot should slide easily up and down, allowing you to adjust the size of the loop.

Furball's Meow

Step 6: Insert a cat toy through the loop and pull the rope tightly. The more I tug on the toy, the more secure the rope will be.

Part Three:
A Greener Cat

Taking Greenventory

To begin greening your Kitty's lifestyle, start by taking a "greenventory" to see where you're at and where you can improve. There are bound to be ample opportunities to reduce your pet's carbon paw print.

Start your green inventory by looking at:

- Toys
- Cat litter and accessories
- Food
- Bedding and scratching posts
- Pet carriers
- Stains and odor control

Greener Toy Choices

While you are strongly encouraged to make your own cat toys, it is highly likely that your diva Kitty may wish to enjoy the occasional store bought toy. Here are some guidelines for making greener choices:

1. Only buy toys that you know Kitty will love. Observe her preferences and stick with them. If she loves one type of toy, keep buying more of the same. This will help reduce the number of discarded toys.

2. Buy quality over quantity. Before you make your purchase, examine the toy to see how well it is made. Does it look sturdy or does it look cheaply made? A quality toy will last longer.

3. Buy locally made toys. You'll help support the local economy and also reduce the resources required to ship the toy to your store. Ideally, the toys should be made from locally sourced materials as well.

4. Choose organic and natural. With the growth in environmental awareness, there are now many options for toys made with organic catnip and natural materials.

5. Stay away from battery operated toys. There is no substitute for the real thing, which is you. Kitty will always find her human companions infinitely more entertaining than a repetitive battery operated toy.

6. Invent your own toys and games. You and Kitty are a fountain of creativity. There are no limits. Just remember to play safely.

Eco-friendly Cat Litter

Probably one of the biggest environmental impacts your Kitty can make is to switch from a clumping clay litter to an eco-friendly alternative. Clumping clay litter is often described in green-friendly language such as "made from natural clay." However, this natural clay is better known in industry jargon as sodium bentonite.

Sodium bentonite can expand several times its size when wet. This makes sodium bentonite popular not just for cat litter, but also for industrial uses such as oil field drilling, sealants and binding iron pellets.

It doesn't take the superior intellect of a cat to deduce that using an eco-friendly alternative is a better green choice than using a non-renewable resource that is strip-mined.

Here are some eco-friendly options for Kitty:

Recycled Newspaper Litter

This litter is manufactured from recycled newspapers. It's composed of grey cylindrical pellets that are about as wide as the slots of a typical litter scoop. It also comes in a softer version which has a crumbly texture. This version is recommended by the manufacturer as a transitional litter if your cat is used to clay.

This was Furball's first litter and it did a good job of keeping odors in check. The only downside was that the pellets would sometimes stick in between his toes and thus, were occasionally found in strange places throughout the house.

Organic Wheatgrass Litter

After moving to the west coast, I switched Furball to organic wheatgrass litter because I couldn't find his regular brand.

This litter's cylindrical pellets are similar in appearance to the recycled newspaper litter. It also does a decent job of handling odors, but has a malted barley smell when poured fresh from the bag.

Wheat Litter

I was enticed to try a wheat litter after a fabulous sales pitch at the San Francisco Green Festival. Unfortunately, Furball wasn't as keen to use the litter. It seemed he wasn't sure whether he should eat the litter or pee in it.

Furball once had a blocked bladder and as a result, I give him lots of water with his food. This also means that he urinates a lot more than the average cat. As a consequence, once he did start using the litter, I found the wheat congealed into heavy bricks and was a bit cumbersome to scoop. However, our neighbor used this litter for her cat and had no issues. The odor control was as good as the other eco-friendly options.

Pine Litter

According to the manufacturer, this type of litter is made from recycled pine. Furball hasn't tried pine litter, but one of his feline friends has. It was reported that the odor control was excellent for urine, but not as good for number two.

Corn Litter

Neither Furball nor his friends have any experience with this type of litter. If you have, please visit Furball's website at **www.greenlittlecat.com** and share your experience. The manufacturer of a popular corn litter states on their website that they use whole kernel corn. As a result, when considering this litter, you may wish to factor in the controversy surrounding biodiesel production raising the price of corn as a food staple.

Litter Box and Scoop

If there's one product that should be made from recycled plastic, litter boxes and scoops are it (okay, that's two products). At the time of writing, there is one major manufacturer leading the way by committing to use at least 25% recycled materials in their products. This is a great start, but shouldn't Kitty's box and scoop be made from 100% recycled plastic? Help this company and their competitors along by writing or emailing to voice your concerns.

Food for Thought

Consider switching to a more eco-friendly cat food. However, you should always consult your cat's veterinarian before making any changes to your cat's diet.

It's also a challenge to determine which food truly is a greener choice. Organic, natural and locally produced ingredients are better for the environment, but how do you know what's the best choice? Start with the food you currently feed Kitty.

Most manufacturers have a website or 1-800 number listed on the package. Give them a call or write to ask where they get their ingredients from and where the food is made. If the ingredients aren't local or organic, tell them how important this issue is to you and Kitty. After the massive pet food recall in 2007, isn't Kitty worth this small effort?

If it's not possible to change Kitty's diet, there are some simple things you can do to help reduce your cat's carbon paw print.

1. If Kitty eats canned food, recycle the tins. This small act can help divert millions of empty cans from landfill sites.

2. Buy the larger sized bag of cat food because it will use slightly less packaging than two smaller bags with the same amount of food. Pour about a week's worth of food into a reusable container (I use a yoghurt tub for Furball) and scoop your cat's daily meals from this container. This way, you'll need to open the bag less often and it will stay fresher longer. Of course, this only makes sense if the food doesn't expire in the time it takes for your cat to finish the bag. Make sure to check the expiry date.

3. Make fewer trips to the pet food store. Pick up an extra bag or a few more cans on your next visit. You'll not only save a trip, you'll save yourself some time. Just remember to check the expiry dates.

Other Products and Accessories

Bedding

There are a growing number of eco-friendly options, especially from small local companies. Dog beds appear to be ahead of the curve, so if you're looking for greener choices, they're a great place to start.

We all know however, that Kitty's favorite place to nap is anywhere there's a sunny spot in the room. If you really want to go green, she'd likely be just as happy on an old towel placed in a sunbeam.

Scratching Posts

The options are somewhat limited for enviro-friendly scratching posts, which means there's a great opportunity to let retailers and manufacturers know that you'd like greener choices. Send a letter to your favorite pet retailer and let them know you'd like to see more eco-friendly products in their stores.

As well, before you buy a replacement scratching post, see if you can extend the life of Kitty's current post. Give it a vacuum and trim off any stray threads. If you're really adventurous, there are numerous instructions on the Internet to make your own scratching post.

Pet Carriers

One of the largest makers of pet carriers offers a product made with 25% recycled content. If Kitty needs a carrier, this would be a great option. Of course, reusing one would be an even greener choice. If you do, make sure the carrier is in excellent condition, clean, safe and the right size for your cat.

Stains and Odor Control

Hopefully your Kitty will never need these products, but if she does, consider natural alternatives before resorting to chemicals. There are many natural products that work just as well as less eco-friendly options.

Baking soda is great for deodorizing litter boxes and nature's air freshener, an open window, works wonders.

Not the Last Word

Furball and I applaud you for making greener choices to reduce your carbon paw print. There's an amazing opportunity for cat owners to vote with their dollars by supporting businesses that respect our environment. Visit Furball's website at **www.greenlittlecat.com** for sample letters to send to retailers and for more ways to take action.

While we might not save the planet with a single cat toy, it can definitely be the first step. So, why not take it? Imagine 60 million furry little paws and 30 million human feet moving forward together.

Go green, little cat!

Toy Index

Toys by Difficulty
1 Paw: Super Easy

Cat Beacon, 65

Cerlox Holmes, 89

Classic Shopping Bag, 32

Crunch and Bunch, 46

Dream Cat-cher, 64

Flying Horseshoes, 37

Go Fish, 107

Hide 'n Peek Bag, 39

Juice Pull, 42

Juicy Hoop, 43

Madcap, 44

Nuts 'n Bolts, 62

Penned Up Energy, 88

Ping Pong Pinball, 54

Ring Toss, 30

Schrodinger's Box, 26

Tubular Tubes, 47

Unwrap This!, 50

Water Bottle Dodgeball, 45

2 Paws: Easy

Biz Card Flicker, 84

Classic Ball of Yarn, 73

Flippity Flappity Flag, 40

Floppy Jacks, 36

Hemp Hula, 70

Houdini's Pendulum, 58

ID Badge, 86

Jingles, the Reindeer, 80

Kitty Broomstick, 90

Lazy Wrestle Sausage, 104

Peek-a-boo House, 28

Polar Ribbon, 108

Ratty Sock on a String, 106

Saturn Rings, 60

Stringkey, 61

Sweep Around, 31

Tape Ball, 38

The Fishing Pole, 56

The Pretzel, 33

The Shaker, 55

Utility Belt, 72

3 Paws: Somewhat Easy

Braided Rope Snake, 34

Candy Rocket, 24

Catnip Bowtie, 110

Firecracker, 96

Pharaoh's Pyramid, 77

Spider Ballet, 68

Tissue Kebab, 48

Whipper Snapper, 76

4 Paws: Slightly Hard

Beanbag Ravioli, 98

Catnip Satchel 101, 94

Rapunzel's Braid, 74

Wrestle Sausage, 101

Toys by Time
1 minute or less

Cat Beacon, 65

Classic Shopping Bag, 32

Crunch and Bunch, 46

Dream Cat-cher, 64

Flippity Flappity Flag, 40

Floppy Jacks, 36

Flying Horseshoes, 37

Go Fish, 107

Hide 'n Peek Bag, 39

Houdini's Pendulum, 58

Jingles, the Reindeer, 80

Juice Pull, 42

Juicy Hoop, 43

Madcap, 44

Nuts 'n Bolts, 62

Penned Up Energy, 88

Ping Pong Pinball, 54

Ratty Sock on a String, 106

Ring Toss, 30
Saturn Rings, 60
Schrodinger's Box, 26
Stringkey, 61
The Pretzel, 33
Tubular Tubes, 47
Water Bottle Dodgeball, 45

2 to 3 minutes

Biz Card Flicker, 84
Catnip Bowtie, 110
Cerlox Holmes, 89
ID Badge, 86
Kitty Broomstick, 90
Lazy Wrestle Sausage, 104
Spider Ballet, 68
Sweep Around, 31
Tape Ball, 38
The Fishing Pole, 56
The Shaker, 55
Unwrap This!, 50

5 to 10 minutes

Braided Rope Snake, 34
Candy Rocket, 24
Classic Ball of Yarn, 73
Firecracker, 96
Hemp Hula, 70

Peek-a-boo House, 28
Pharaoh's Pyramid, 77
Polar Ribbon, 108
Tissue Kebab, 48
Utility Belt, 72

Over 10 minutes

Beanbag Ravioli, 98
Catnip Satchel 101, 94
Rapunzel's Braid, 74
Whipper Snapper, 76
Wrestle Sausage, 101

Toys by Play Category

Catch

Beanbag Ravioli, 98
Biz Card Flicker, 84
Braided Rope Snake, 34
Candy Rocket, 24
Cat Beacon, 65
Catnip Bowtie, 110
Catnip Satchel 101, 94
Crunch and Bunch, 46
Flippity Flappity Flag, 40
Floppy Jacks, 36
Flying Horseshoes, 37

Go Fish, 107
Hemp Hula, 70
Houdini's Pendulum, 58
ID Badge, 86
Jingles, the Reindeer, 80
Juice Pull, 42
Juicy Hoop, 43
Pharaoh's Pyramid, 77
Polar Ribbon, 108
Rapunzel's Braid, 74
Ratty Sock on a String, 106
Ring Toss, 30
Saturn Rings, 60
Spider Ballet, 68
Sweep Around, 31
Tape Ball, 38
The Fishing Pole, 56
The Pretzel, 33
Utility Belt, 72
Whipper Snapper, 76

Chase

Beanbag Ravioli, 98
Biz Card Flicker, 84
Candy Rocket, 24
Cat Beacon, 65
Catnip Bowtie, 110
Catnip Satchel 101, 94

Cerlox Holmes, 89

Classic Ball of Yarn, 73

Crunch and Bunch, 46

Dream Cat-cher, 64

Flippity Flappity Flag, 40

Flying Horseshoes, 37

Hemp Hula, 70

Houdini's Pendulum, 58

Jingles, the Reindeer, 80

Juicy Hoop, 43

Madcap, 44

Nuts 'n Bolts, 62

Penned Up Energy, 88

Ping Pong Pinball, 54

Saturn Rings, 60

Sweep Around, 31

Tape Ball, 38

The Fishing Pole, 56

The Pretzel, 33

The Shaker, 55

Tubular Tubes, 47

Water Bottle Dodgeball, 45

Stalk

Cat Beacon, 65

Classic Shopping Bag, 32

Dream Cat-cher, 64

Hide 'n Peek Bag, 39

Houdini's Pendulum, 58

ID Badge, 86

Juicy Hoop, 43

Kitty Broomstick, 90

Peek-a-boo House, 28

Penned Up Energy, 88

Ratty Sock on a String, 106

Schrodinger's Box, 26

Stringkey, 61

The Fishing Pole, 56

Tissue Kebab, 48

Unwrap This!, 50

Wrestle

Braided Rope Snake, 34

Catnip Bowtie, 110

Catnip Satchel 101, 94

Firecracker, 96

Go Fish, 107

Lazy Wrestle Sausage, 104

Polar Ribbon, 108

Rapunzel's Braid, 74

Ratty Sock on a String, 106

Spider Ballet, 68

The Fishing Pole, 56

Utility Belt, 72

Whipper Snapper, 76

Wrestle Sausage, 101

Lazy Cat

Braided Rope Snake, 34

Go Fish, 107

Houdini's Pendulum, 58

ID Badge, 86

Juice Pull, 42

Polar Ribbon, 108

Rapunzel's Braid, 74

Ratty Sock on a String, 106

Spider Ballet, 68

Stringkey, 61

The Fishing Pole, 56

Tissue Kebab, 48

Utility Belt, 72

Whipper Snapper, 76

About the Author

Holly Tse lives in Northern California with her husband and Furball. She is a lifelong environmentalist and has been promoting green causes since she was seven years old and wrote the government to ask what they were doing to stop acid rain.

She is also an ardent cat lover and has spent hundreds of hours playing with cats. She is somewhat abashed to admit this number is probably closer to 2000 hours or 83 full days of her life.

Make Your Own Cat Toys is her first self-published book. She also enjoyed drawing the illustrations and designing the cover for this title.

About Furball

Furball's favorite activities are eating, napping and playing. He lives a green west coast lifestyle. *Make Your Own Cat Toys* is the first book to be written about him and he expects many more to follow.

For more eco-friendly tips and to stay up on Furball's antics, please visit his website at: **www.greenlittlecat.com**.

27245445R00076

Made in the USA
San Bernardino, CA
09 December 2015